BIG WALLS

BIG WALLS

BREAKTHROUGHS ON THE FREE-CLIMBING FRONTIER

PAUL PIANA

PHOTOGRAPHS BY
GALEN ROWELL
BILL HATCHER
BETH WALD

FOREWORD BY
ROYAL ROBBINS

A SIERRA CLUB BOOK

The Sierra Club, founded in 1892 by John Muir, has devoted itself to the study
and protection of the Earth's scenic and ecological resources—mountains, wet-
lands, woodlands, wild shores and rivers, deserts and plains. The publishing program of the Sierra Club offers books to the public as a nonprofit educational
service in the hope that they may enlarge the public's understanding of the Club's
basic concerns. The point of view expressed in each book, however, does not nec-
essarily represent that of the Club. The Sierra Club has some sixty chapters coast
to coast, in Canada, Hawaii, and Alaska. For information about how you may participate in its programs to preserve wilderness and the quality of life, please
address inquiries to Sierra Club, 85 Second Street, San Francisco, CA 94109.
Web address: http://www.sierraclub.org/books

LIBRARY OF CONGRESS CALALOGING-IN-PUBLICATION DATA
Piana, Paul.
   Big walls : breakthroughs on the free-climbing frontier / Paul
Piana.
      p.   cm.
   ISBN 0-87156-960-4 (alk. paper)
   1. Free climbing.   2. Piana, Paul.   3. Mountaineers—United
States—Biography.   I. Title.
GV200.25.P53 1997
796.52'23—dc21
                                                97-7405
                                                CIP

Production by Janet Vail and Robin Rockey
Book and jacket design by Paula Schlosser

Printed in Singapore

10 9 8 7 6 5 4 3 2 1

This book is dedicated to my greatest heroes.

To my dad, James A. Piana.

He is the living example of "the harder you try, the luckier you get." For the sacrifices he has made for my family, beginning as a young boy in the Depression, as a soldier in World War II, and later as a tremendous father and role model. Dad is my greatest hero of all.

To the late Paul Muehl.

Since 1971 Paul dragged and coaxed me up impossible climbs, taught me so many things including that it is important to think and not merely to have an opinion. Best of all, he was a great friend. Even though his passing has left a vast and empty place in the world, he is with me every day and on every climb.

CONTENTS

September 1961, Royal Robbins, Chuck Pratt and Tom Frost (L-R), are hiking down from the summit of El Capitan, having made the first ascent of the Salathé Wall, which was by far the most difficult rock climb in the world. In ancient Greece, the Olympic victors were crowned with laurel leaves. Fittingly, these champions, whose greatest reward is nothing more or less than the first ascent of the "world's greatest rock climb," were playfully crowned with summer blossoms. Even though the equipment they used was 1961 state-of-the-art, this photo conveys how different was the game. They are carrying everything they had with them on the climb—very little hardware, no ascenders, no bivouac gear or specialized clothing and certainly no hope of rescue if things went awry.

FOREWORD

BY ROYAL ROBBINS

BEFORE THE DEED COMES the thought. Before the achievement comes the dream. Every mountain we climb, we first climb in our mind. This book is a story of wildest dreams and their realization, of dreams and the way they come to bear fruit. The dreams that are the subject of this book were bold to the point of audacity: the ascents of four North American premier big walls in a style unimaginable to the climbers who made the first ascents. What style? It's called "free climbing." It means using only the natural features of the rock for upward progress. The first ascents of these walls all involved substantial amounts (well more than fifty percent) of what we call direct-aid climbing, involving the use of pitons or other gadgets for upward movement via short rope ladders. The men who made the first ascents of these walls were dreamers, too, but they never dreamed the climbs they had spent so much time making with direct aid would ever go "free." That was left to more modern visionaries.

Two such were Paul Piana and his longtime climbing partner, Todd Skinner, two remarkable young men from Lander, Wyoming. Over the years they have become one of the most productive teams to blaze trails in the mountains. And they have specialized in free climbing.

Free climbing has a long and honorable history in American mountaineering. The first free ascents of routes that have previously required direct aid are prizes sought after by climbers eager to do something new, to make a type of "first ascent." In Yosemite, route after route that had long been an aid climb has succumbed to the disciplined efforts of talented and tenacious climbers with the single goal of doing what no one has done before. Some of the prominent Yosemite climbs where aid has been eliminated include the North Face of Sentinel Rock, the Lost Arrow, the North West Face of Half Dome, and the East Face of the Washington Column (now known as Astro Man).

IN THIS BOOK PAUL PIANA tells the tale of free climbing four renowned precipices in North America, walls of which I was fortunate enough, along with friends who were equal partners, to have made the first ascents. If anyone had asked me if any of these climbs would ever go free, I would have answered, "Of course not!" The reason why nobody ever asked is that no one *dreamed* of freeing these routes until years after the original ascents. Eventually the unimaginable began to be conceived, and eventually dreams became reality. I am happy to have been wrong about the "impossibility" of free climbing these walls. Although it is a comment upon the limits of my vision, it is even more a tribute to the two men who made the impossible come true.

Piana and Skinner weren't the only ones to dream, but they were the most persistent—especially Skinner, whose dogged refusal to give up on Half Dome suggests a steadfastness bordering on obstinacy.

But, this is Paul's book, and these are his tales to tell, and he tells them well indeed. This is a book of uplift, of light, and of color. The only thing that mars the story (though not the book) was the casting of doubt by the climbing press and some leading members of the climbing community on the pair's free ascent of the Salathé Wall. This was not the climbing community's best hour. Then, when the German Alex Huber made the second free ascent, in effect vindicating Piana and Skinner's claim by showing that the route *could* be done, Huber and his partner claimed that, because of certain technicalities, the Wyoming duo's ascent didn't count, even if they did climb it "free." This is a little like claiming that the second ascent of El Capitan, which was done in one seven-day push, was really a first ascent because the first party used fixed ropes.

These controversies make me a bit sad. They show what happens when hubris overcomes the brotherhood of the rope.

Although our climbing philosophies hardly overlap, my personal experience with Piana and Skinner is quite refreshing. I like and admire them for several reasons. First, in their climbs, they have shown, besides technical skill, a trait I much admire that is aptly described by an old-fashioned American word: *grit*. They've got the spirit. They hang in there. They don't give up. Second, they love climbing, just in itself. Their pure joy in moving up rock, apart from accomplishment, is palpable. They also have some other traits that evoke admiration. One is their lively sense of humor, which expresses itself in their ability to laugh at themselves and to take neither themselves nor their climbs too seriously. They are open, and friendly, and cheerful. And they live and climb with boundless enthusiasm. I guess, at heart, they are just old-fashioned, optimistic American entrepreneurs.

In this book are fine stories of optimistic enterprise. Have a good read!

INTRODUCTION

B*IG WALLS* IS A STORY about dreams come true. It is a story about wild climbs and great memories. In many ways it is the story of the end of one era's climbing style and the beginning of another.

When we look back on our adventures, we can say that we saw the stylistic changes coming, but more accurately *we were* the changes—we were striving, climbing, and having rich fun while living the good, high life on cliffs both large and small. As the climbing world looks back, the ink on paper that is history seems sudden and profound, but for us it was a gradual and logical path—it was climbing.

Big Walls is a book about four big walls and two rock climbers who, at first, and only in their dreams, put themselves in the places of their climbing heroes, and about two friends who realized that they had the talent, tenacity, and strength to achieve these climbs.

Paul Piana and Todd Skinner on the 5.13b final Headwall pitch of the Salathé Wall, El Capitan, Yosemite Valley, California. Paul is seen leading the pinky/ring finger–thin crack which begins the last of four 5.13 pitches on the Free Salathé.

This book is about Todd Skinner and me. It is about the adventures we have shared in making the first free climbs of the four premier big walls in North America. Free climbing these four big walls was the culmination of many years of experience, training, and then trying and trying and trying . . . until finally we could succeed.

To succeed in free climbing big walls, we first had to learn how to free climb the little walls. Many years ago, we were already enamored with the joys of climbing—with an awareness that the more energy we put into it, the more personal rewards we experienced. While Todd and I would wile away winter hours by climbing on a tiny block wall in the basement of the University of Wyoming at Laramie, we would philosophize about what was most important to us about climbing. Both of us had read many books about the great climbers and their climbs. We admired those who were brave enough to heed their instincts and to adapt a prior generation's style of ascent to make new achievements possible. When we were old men and retired, we wanted, just like our heroes, to have experienced great adventures. We wanted to make important first ascents.

As a young boy in the shadows of Wyoming's Wind River Mountains, Todd and his older brother were taken on snow and rock climbs by their father who, during the 1950s, had done a lot of climbing with Dick and Bill Long. A first ascent of Yosemite's Middle Cathedral Rock, the third ascent of Shiprock, and several important ascents in the Bellacoola Range of British Columbia were the source of Todd's youngest dreams—born while listening to grand retellings around climbers' campfires.

I grew up away from the big mountains, on the western edge of the Black Hills and, from the outset, my focus was on rock climbing. During my early years (as well as to this day), my inspiration came from two climbers who, in the late '40s, "dropped out" of a normal lifestyle and climbed their way around the western United States. On their way to Devils Tower, Herb and Jan Conn discovered the paradise that caused them to abandon their peripatetic quest—or at least to confine it within the Black Hills, where they climbed daily, as Herb wrote, "like two cats in an unattended fish market," making hundreds of first ascents.

As a result of the influences by books about climbs and adventures, as well as by colorful, firsthand accounts of thrilling first ascents, we began our search for similar experiences. Some of the following vignettes provide impressions of our up-and-coming days as climbers.

CERBERUS, 1970:

I climbed for several years before I first met real climbers. This pinnacle stands near the Needles Highway. As a novice, I couldn't imagine a human climbing anything so impossible looking, yet, high above the ground, I could see equipment in the rock, and it had to have gotten there somehow!

During the late '60s, whenever we could persuade someone's parents to drive us to the Needles, my junior high buddies and I used to scramble up a flake just across from Cerberus (5.8) to gaze across at the sheer impossibility of climbing the thing. We could see a couple of piton placements and two bolts high up, but little that we recognized as hand holds. We knew that some guy from California, with the unlikely-sounding name of Royal Robbins, had first climbed it. By talking to Herb and Jan Conn, we also found out that a character from my hometown of Newcastle, Wyoming, had repeated the climb. I sought out Renn Fenton and pestered him until he agreed to take me climbing.

Whether or not Renn actually believed in my ability, it never crossed his mind that one shouldn't try. He often suggested that I tie in and lead. Renn showed me better ways to tie in, utilizing knots that real climbers used.

Once, after sneaking through the woods to spy on John Gill, and watch him climb from a distance, I arrived back in Newcastle with questions about what I had seen: amazing climbing and a small, mysterious white block. Renn took me to the drugstore and, for twenty-five cents, I was the proud owner of a block of the substance that I had reported seeing Gill use on his hands. Renn suggested that not only was it effective to rub the block of chalk on my hands for improved grip on boulder problems, but that it might come in handy on longer climbs as well. "Just smash it up and put some in your pockets," he advised.

Cramming half a block into the pockets of my snug and fashionable hip-hugger, bell-bottom Levis, I climbed up the start of Cerberus, pausing to hammer in a couple of CMI Off-sets. Ten feet higher, I decided to see if this chalk stuff worked

Every climber has a spiritual home, and for Paul Piana it is the Black Hills of South Dakota.

on long climbs as well as it did on the boulders. I fought to force my hand into the taut seam that was my pocket, never pausing to think that once I got my hand in there, I might not be able to get it out . . . which of course was the case! After what seemed like an hour of panic and struggle to extricate my hand, I fell off and soared into the Black Hills sky. It was terrifying. After a fair bit of blurring rock, laughing Renn's skillful belay stopped me—hand in pocket. I never again made such a bad choice in climbing garments.

A year later, in 1970, on a particularly memorable day, I realized we were, once again, walking to the base of Cerberus. With Renn's confidence bolstering me, I fluidly led what for me had been only a dream climb. The ease with which I made that ascent is still one of the highlights of my climbing career, as it was a major psychological revelation.

4TH OF JULY CRACK, 1980 AND 1981:

This climb was very important to both Todd and me, because it was the first of many difficult climbs we worked on together, and was the beginning of our long history as a climbing team.

This Vedauwoo climb had been the object of several strong attempts by visiting Colorodan and eastern climbers. It was rumored that if it was free-climbable, the 4th of July Crack would certainly bear the then-mythical rating of 5.12. We had talked about it for a few weeks and Todd had the first opportunity to try. He spent a number of afternoons after classes trying to work out the first crux.

When we went to the 4th of July Crack together, my greater experience and larger repertory of moves allowed me to quickly figure out how to do the tricky, flaring jams, and to find two outrageous bridging moves between knobs, and a rest, of sorts. Even so, we spent six days on this climb before being able to free climb it. On the lucky day, I slipped and fell, a move from the home free alcove. On Todd's turn, he began with the

Hundreds of pinnacles rising like cities of stone from rolling hillsides of Ponderosa Pine offer both a challenging vertical arena and a beautifully unique playground for climbers. Paul is seen making the 1990 first ascent of "Forbidden Colors" (5.13a), one of his favorite climbs.

jitters, thrutching upward, but as he climbed higher, he moved more smoothly with increasing concentration and skill. When Todd pulled over the top, we had not only completed our premiere 5.12 first ascent and the first climb of that grade in the state of Wyoming, but Todd had emerged as an equal partner. Neither of us looked back.

ELEVEN-CENT MOON, 1981:

Eleven-Cent Moon is an important route, not only because of its difficulty, but because it taught us that our vision was on track and that these climbs were indeed possible for us. It was an early 5.12 that, due to changes in equipment and attitude, slipped down the scale to 5.11d. Nevertheless, it is probably the highest quality new route we climbed together during our Vedauwoo years.

When the evening sun skids across this flat wall, its formerly invisible flakes are held in relief, and thousands of jet shadows spangle the wall. At this hour, the whiplash of Eleven-Cent Moon's upper dihedral is as strikingly beautiful as any climb I have seen. Looking across Vedauwoo Glen from 4th of July Crack, this line courts any rock climber.

The last twenty-five feet involved spooky fingertip laybacking. Here, I could wiggle in Chouinard #1 stoppers: frail, cabled flecks of aluminum which the Chouinard brochure claimed would hold short falls. Even though the crack was so shallow at that point as to allow only 3/4 of the tiny stoppers to be inserted, I believed the brochure, having taken very short drops on them. I wiggled two of the threadlike pieces of "protection" into the crack.

As the dihedral curved over my head and the laybacking became desperate, the crack pinched down even more. The little stoppers were six or seven feet below my quivering EB climbing shoes. Looking down and seeing 1/4 of each stopper sticking out instantly sapped all of my confidence, and despair gained tons in the pit of my stomach. Two moves above my head, the fissure was almost a roof crack, yet it widened into what looked like a bomber fingerlock. Two grams of hope overcame the tons of despair and made my decision to go for glory.

In May 1980, Todd and Paul made the first free ascent of Vedauwoo's 4th of July Crack, which, at 5.12a, was the first climb of that grade in Wyoming. Initially we climbed it by following the route of the aid ascents, which was to belay in a niche near the top, then traverse right and climb the last bit of Horn's Mother (the crack system just to the right). Subsequent ascents have climbed straight to the top rather than traversing. In 1981, after a trip to Yosemite (during which we climbed Separate Reality, Tales of Power, and HangDog Flyer, among others), Todd counted coup with the first red point of the climb and its second free ascent. This was one of the most important routes in our history as a climbing team.

Todd Skinner is "keeping it together" on a very serious lead on Devils Tower in Wyoming. During the pre-sport climbing, thin-crack era, Todd and Paul considered Devils Tower to be one of the most significant climbing arenas.

Everything was going wrong, yet I was still climbing. My fingertips were brushing the bomber fingerlock as I kicked my left foot high up toward a smear more perfect than any from the McCarthy era. Suddenly I was no longer moving slowly upward but was transformed into a supersonic blur, rocketing down the wall . . . not feeling, but hearing the *schick-schick* of #1 stopper cables breaking. A thirty-foot, hour-long second later, Bob Cowan's solid belay and a bolt I had placed far below, checked my fall. Bob, who had recently taken to wearing a mustache and goatee, looked as shocked as Robert E. Lee after Appomattox. He did not want to resume the battle.

Two days after, Bob and Todd worked on the climb with top-ropes, but were unable to make it through the crux section to the fingerlock. I had driven south to Ft. Collins, Colorado, and had been elated to see items that became a protection godsend. RPs are an Australian product designed to fit into thin, shallow cracks, and are much stronger than like-sized Chouinard stoppers. Realizing the RPs' potential, I immediately bought a set and drove straight to Vedauwoo, encountering Todd and Bob, who had just pulled their top-ropes after another day of failing to get through the crux. Tying in immediately, and with the confidence provided by this new form of protection, I quickly led the pitch, making the route's first free ascent.

In 1985, for protection during this 5.12 first ascent of Hollow Men, Todd placed 14 #1 RPs in a row. (A #1 RP is a cabled loop with a tiny brass wedge on one end. The wedge is similar in size and shape to a paper match head.) With protection that insubstantial, it's a good thing he didn't fall.

THE GUNFIGHTER, 1984:

The Gunfighter (5.13b) is a significant route for Todd, since it was the first time he had established a route of 5.13 difficulty. The psychological rather than the physical breakthrough represented by this route was probably more significant for Todd. During our first visit to Hueco in 1982, we had hiked to the base of what would become known as The Gunfighter, but only gazed

longingly at the potential it represented. The following entries from Todd's journal record the history of the first ascent of this landmark climb.

5/9 — It's really hot down here—shade routes only. Today I was back on what will be known as The Gunfighter. So damn hard!!! I got the rope up quite a ways today, but at one point, reached behind me to grab a Friend and ended up with my chalkbag in my teeth and no more strength left in either hand!

5/13 — I failed again yesterday and today would have been an appropriate day to have outdrawn The Gunfighter but I got shot down again. Today I got a special package in the mail. We were just sitting around discussing the need for a super-fast method of chalking up, when up drives the Ranger with a large envelope. Piana has sent an around-the-neck, slap-activated, chalk-banger! Invented especially for this climb, it works really well and I'm sure we'll be able to apply the theory on other desperadoes.

I almost gave up today, because I couldn't find a logical way to do the last grim moves, nor a good way to get to them. I tried everything from lunges to double heel-hooks, to hand-against-foot stacks! Finally, at wits' end, I connected wild lunges and opposition holds and made the moves. So, so, so Hard!

5/14 — I took a day off and did some soloing and a new, beautiful two pitch face route on the main face that went at 5.10+X.

5/15 — Tenth day on The Gunfighter and I almost got it!!! Power failure just inches from the end. It was heartbreaking, but now I know I'll get it soon. I found an over-the-head knee-lock that connects crux sections. The route is so unendingly technical and terminally sustained! Near end of page—leaving space for good news . . .

5/17 — Bad News. I came really close today but could not stick on the last dyno move. All out with the right hand for a rounded bump that is so hard to get and harder to stay on. I went up today from the ground. Until now, I've left the ropes up but don't want any questions regarding validity when this is finished.

Yesterday, Ernest Cisneros and I were throwing knives and Ernest was seriously wounded, so a climber named Dave and I

Todd's first ascent of The Gunfighter was prior to sport climbing's focus on overhanging face climbing skills. As a crack/face hybrid, this gymnastic route employed "tricky, bouldering style body-english," not common on climbs until a decade later. In addition

to taping his hands as protection against rasp-like hand jams, Todd has taped his leg to facilitate a clever calf-hook—utilizing his calf somewhat like a third hand. Todd returned to this climb many times in 1984, and that spring, he swaggered away having outdrawn the Gunfighter.

did a much sought-after, direct finish to Indecent Exposure. It was a hard 5.11 facing a thirty-foot fall, then a great Friend, then fifteen feet to a really poor Stopper. I could have down-climbed to the Friend, so I went up on a scouting effort to see how the rest would go. It was all overhanging but had good holds. Fifteen feet out from the nut, I suddenly committed to a lay away sequence that I couldn't reverse. I started going for it wildly and everything was slanted and sloping and about then the Stopper fell out. The old Fire's paid for themselves about then with a stand on a vertical dish to enable a fast hand switch and a lunge to a better hold. Twenty feet more of 5.10 and

twenty more of 5.9 to the belay. I was, naturally, praying that nothing would break near the top. Dark Horse, 5.11X.

5/18 — Waiting for a partner on a hot morning. I hope it goes today. Four strong attempts, but no gold. I'm being belayed by Son-of-Judge. Three-hour nap between first and last pair of attempts. Lonely bivvy and psyche out/up.

5/19 — A long fall trying to clip in with slack in my hand. I hurt my right hand—I stayed out and psyched all day in the desert. When I came in, I found a girl to belay me. No Mistakes. The Gunfighter, 5.13!!! Adios Amigo!

When Legends Die (5.13a) is one of Todd's favorite first ascents. The first and most difficult moves are well protected, but the final 5.12a moves are not.

Todd once wrote to Paul: "At the last moves, which are about 5.12a, you can fall forty feet! You cannot see anything of the route below you. It just rounds into oblivion, and since you have traversed out over the desert, you're 200 feet off the ground — it's so cool. There you're ready for air time! It's safe but you get quite a tantalizing effect!"

WHEN LEGENDS DIE, 1987:

When Legends Die (5.13a/b) is a tremendous climb Todd established in 1987. The following is taken from an excited letter he wrote to me a day or two after the first ascent.

John Sherman was in Australia and had written us a letter telling us about a route at Arapiles called Punks in the Gym. He said it's as steep and looks like The Gunfighter but without the crack! We laughed!

Russel Erickson found When Legends Die and we sort of looked at it and laughed again. We thought it, too, would be like The Gunfighter without the crack. Russel rapped it and got all excited and badgered us until finally, we rapped it.

The crux, we thought would be high up—where it wasn't. The crux turned out to be the first twenty feet, and is a dynamic move and I'm really lousy with those. It's a B-1 entry into a 5.12+.

A very talented Belgian climber, Arnould T'Kint, in repeating the climb, said it was the best route he'd done in America. The top part of the climb is silver rock. It's the best of all. Beautiful rock with edges coming out of it. You can't believe it—the whole thing overhangs. Near the top is a section we called the slab which is about 100 degrees. It's the last thirty feet and at the end, you can take a thirty-footer. At the last move, if you're pumped and blow it, you can fall up to forty feet! We left it as a runout simply to add spice! When you look down from the last dicey moves, which are about 5.12a, you see nothing! You cannot see anything of the route below you. It just rounds into oblivion and since you have traversed out over the desert, you're 200 feet off the ground—it's so cool. So there you're ready for air time!

You'll disappear! It's safe but you get quite a tantalizing effect!

We named every hold! it was fun to work on it and to have all these colorful places to attain! . . . you come out of the undercling into the peanut and then you get to El Niño. Ariel was named after the owner of the quanset hut we lived in, because the hold is pretty nice looking but it's pretty useless. Out of that is the second crux and a really hard clip. The only one to really fall out of control at that point was Mark Sonnenfeld, and he hurt Bill Myers, who was belaying him. Mark is such a big lad and Bill wasn't at the end of his tether. He just got splattered! Mark took a twenty-footer but on this route you can take twenty-footers anywhere—.

The route took me four days to work out. I had wired the top but couldn't do the bottom dyno! When I finally did the move, I did the rest of the route, but I've only done that one move that one time! I'm the worst at moves like that—it's powerful and long and when you hit, you have to stick this sloper. For me, that's the worst combination of all. Even so, I was a little depressed when I got it. The year before, when we found it, we thought it would be a candidate for 5.13d but as it turns out it's much easier, so I was pretty bummed out. It turned out that we found a 5.11d way to do a pumping 5.12c move and that made the whole climb a lot easier and fall into place faster.

But no matter what the final grade turns out to be, it will never detract from the perfect beauty of the climb! When Legends Die is the best route I've ever done!

High above the celadon waters of Fremont Canyon, Wyoming, Todd is engaged with the crazy-thin crux moves of Psychadelic Psycho (5.12c). He is belayed by the route's first ascentionist, our friend Steve "Nitro" Petro.

Every endeavor has to begin somewhere. For Todd and me, our quest to free climb the four big walls that are the focus of this book began on the little walls of Wyoming, the Black Hills, Hueco Tanks, Texas, and on myriad cliffs across America and Europe. These disparate climbing areas taught us a lot about how to climb, and even more about ourselves. The preceding stories describe climbs significant to our development as climbers and climbing partners. These early adventures served to intensify the drive we felt to see as much of the climbing world as we could, and to make our own contributions to the game.

Our greatest aesthetic contribution to the sport is to free

In this photo of Paul Piana being belayed by his wife Heidi Badaracco, many characteristics blend together: vibrant colors, purity of line, athletic movement, a great partner, and a lovely setting. The climb is the first ascent of Snakebite Evangelist (5.13a) in the Black Hills of South Dakota.

Most climbers are drawn to climbs that offer more than just an upward path. At times, the allure might be a knife-sharp arete or ridge; another might be the geometric purity of a single crack splitting a blank granite slab.

climb the big walls that in the past had been aid climbed. Our experiences gained by establishing some of the most difficult short climbs in America compelled us to believe that it was possible to free climb, rather than merely aid climb, these great walls. Prior to our free climbs of these big walls, climbers had believed it necessary to pound in pitons, to insert nuts, or to set various crack camming gadgets, to which are attached short rope ladders. From the top rung of these ladders, aid climbers then reach higher, inserting another piece of equipment, repeating this process again and again. Ascending in this fashion, climbers were relying completely on their equipment to make upward progress. This is called *aid climbing*.

At one time, this was the only means of climbing these big walls, but improved equipment and training and refined attitudes made it obvious to Todd and me that we could improve on previous ascents by using our hands and feet to ascend the rock in a more pure fashion. We rejected any aid from equipment—we wouldn't use it to pull ourselves up, nor would we hang from it in order to rest. We would utilize our ropes and equipment only for safety. Rather than relying on nylon ladders and hardware to climb these sheer walls, we would utilize only the strength in our hands and the creativity in our minds.

Whereas an aid climber hangs his way upward and is resting on every placement of equipment, a free climber is charged with the task of eliminating that support. With aid climbing, upward progress is always possible, but in free climbing, this is not the case. During an aid climb, if the cracks run out or become unsuitable for further placement of aiding equipment, a hole can be drilled to insert a bolt; not for safety, but so that upward progress may continue.

TODD AND I BELIEVE THAT it is imperative to climb free from the aid of equipment. Using climbing equipment only as our safety net, our goal is to rely solely on the strengths of our bodies and the vagaries of the rock to reach the top. Anything less—utilizing even one rest or using aid to pass a blank, four-foot stretch of rock—means that it is not a free climb.

We were lucky to be climbing at a time when the greatest big walls in North America were just waiting to be free climbed. We were fortunate to realize that the harder you try, the luckier you get. Our gifts of imagination, athleticism, and strength were combined with motivation and tenacity to accomplish new heights in climbing: free ascents of big walls.

We were also aware that our heroes often were criticized by some of the climbers of their day for utilizing new techniques, ideas, and attitudes. We could see that sometimes this criticism was rather harsh and probably caused a fair amount of anguish. However, while we were aware of the criticism our predecessors received, we also saw that they were the ones up on the frontier, risking injury, failure, and criticism. They were also the ones who were making the significant advancements. While our heroes were trying their hardest and fighting gravity, their detractors had stopped climbing to watch from the ground. The greatest climbers rejected the doubt and the ire. They were out there, climbing and climbing and climbing. They were struggling upward and onward, each success building a strength necessary to succeed on another challenge. Our heroes were the ones having all the fun. In short, the best climbers had dared to try. They never gave up. With each climb, their confidence grew and success became a habit.

We realized all of this. Todd and I were determined to revel not only in the love we had for climbing, but also in the thrill of being high up, "pushing the envelope" of our abilities. Some have taken exception to our motivations, to our methods, to our choice of climbs, and even to how much fun we always seem to have. But while critics stand on the ground, we are struggling with the crux of an extreme sport climb in

Wyoming, or trying to remain calm, too far above poor protection in the Black Hills Needles, or enduring the pain of a rasp-like fingerlock on the first free ascent of yet another big wall.

We knew long, long ago that we wanted to be climbers. We wanted to climb new routes and to feel good about ourselves far above the everyday concerns of the rest of the world. We knew that we wanted to possess the confidence of those in the old black-and-white photos we admired. Somewhere along the way we became the climbers of our dreams, but we didn't have the time to realize it because we were too busy climbing an overhanging bulge or mustering the endurance to make one more flaring jam. Today we are still out there climbing. We constantly revel in being high, wild, and free.

FREE CLIMBING ON BIG WALLS:
THE EVOLUTION OF A SPORT

The Renegade (5.13b/c), still one of the most difficult thin cracks in America, caused quite a stir when it was climbed. Certain Yosemite locals thought it unfair that Todd ascended a rope fixed from above, placed a few pitons for protection, and also utilized the then-controversial tactic of "hang-dogging" to learn the moves. This climb rises directly out of an old roadbed and is both prominent and visually striking. As an aid climb it was called The Stigma. Hundreds of pitons were driven and redriven by aid climbers standing in stirrups clipped to each piton placed. The message seemed to be: It is okay to hang from a lot of pounded pitons so that more can be driven and hung upon; it is unfair, however, to selectively place a few pitons to provide protection to free climb the crack. The Renegade was one of the first clashes between what the climbing press dubbed The Traditionalists vs. The Modernists. Ironically, the route has since been bolted by Yosemite locals.

B*IG WALLS.* TO CLIMBERS from around the world, these words evoke images of the tallest, most impossibly smooth rock faces on the planet. To a connoisseur of big wall climbs, only the tallest, sheerest, most monolithic faces hold any interest. Mountains like Everest and walls like The Eiger are dismissed as too easy by those who might be contenders within a modern free climbing arena.

In addition, even though snow, ice, alpine, and rock climbing are members of the mountaineering family tree, they have evolved to the point where they are recognized as being independent disciplines. The most perfect example of a big wall is one of the world's largest granite cliffs, El Capitan, which rises next to the road within Yosemite National Park in California. Due to El Capitan's immensity and proximity to the pavement, several revolutions in climbing attitudes and techniques have taken place upon its walls.

During the early 1960s, while the media turned its attention toward Americans on Everest, the Big Wall revolution was in full swing. Unsung by the media, a small cadre of Americans were revolutionizing climbing by inventing and implementing new climbing techniques. Often snubbed and sometimes reviled by their era's traditionalist climbers, these "mere rock technicians" were busily applying their newfound skills to the most obvious challenges within their climbing world. Typical of any revolution, climbers from the previous generation

Of all the great climbers America has produced, Royal Robbins, the most influential American climber of the 1960s, is probably foremost on any climber's list of heroes. Royal's visionary eye for a climb, tremendous skill, and his incredible drive is manifested in what is perhaps the most enviable first ascent list of any climber, anywhere. Not only did Royal Robbins make significant contributions with new climbs and techniques, but his writings served to spur other climbers to be their best. Royal Robbins always stresses the importance of the spirit behind an adventure and the style with which it is undertaken. In this photo, Royal is seen negotiating a small roof on the third pitch during the first ascent of the Salathé Wall in 1961.

were finding that it is a hard thing to accept that the past one created is directing a future one cannot escape.

Beginning after World War II, climbers began developing new techniques, equipment, and attitudes to ascend these imposing big walls. Yosemite rock climbers approached these walls in much the same way that the postwar mountain climbers approached Everest and the other 8,000-meter peaks—that is, almost anything was fair if it resulted in the attainment of the summit: fixed ropes, huge assault teams, reliance upon equipment for upward progress, and so forth.

El Capitan, Half Dome, Mount Hooker, and Mount Proboscis (all requiring then-state-of-the-art innovations and skills), were climbed around the same period of the first American ascent of Mount Everest. The driving force behind this push to ascend these sheer faces was Royal Robbins, a Californian who had forsaken a "normal" lifestyle to travel all of North America and Europe, seeking out and making the first ascents of what were the world's most technically difficult routes. Robbins was joined in his quest by an elite group of equally driven friends and contemporaries: Chuck Pratt, Tom Frost, Joe Fitschen, Yvon Chouinard, T. M. Herbert, Layton Kor, Glen Denny, Steve Roper, Warren Harding, and others.

THESE CLIMBERS WERE VERY concerned not only with succeeding, but with the style in which the climb was made. As a result, the manner by which they established these landmark climbs evolved along with their growing levels of experience and their belief in what was possible. Prior to the Royal Robbins era, it was widely believed that these big walls were unclimbable. Royal Robbins, Tom Frost, and the other climbers listed above refined older techniques and created new ones and utilized them to bring into being these magnificent aid climbs. Because they had neither the modern equipment nor the modern belief that it is possible to free climb these big walls, these aid-climbing pioneers imposed strict rules upon the game they were creating.

It was obvious to them that by drilling bolts, any section of rock could be aid climbed. The result of this thinking was that they created a widely held rule that bolting was to be done only as a last resort. They would go to tremendous lengths to avoid drilling in bolts. This resulted in long strings of pitons, skillfully tapped into shallow seams in the granite, each one just barely supporting a climber's body weight. They took great pride in crafting scarier and scarier climbs of this nature. However, if the string of poor pitons became too long and the consequence of a fall too horrifying, or if the crack system ended and the option was either to bolt or to retreat, then bolts were placed to allow the climb to continue.

In an aid-climbing context—the only way feasible until very recently—this made perfect sense. One utilized technology for progress, and the goal was to make rules that kept big wall aid climbing challenging within the confines of that particular game. In the game Todd and I have chosen to play (big wall free climbing), it is fair to utilize technology (ropes, pitons, bolts, nuts, etc.) for protection, but not to ensure that the summit is reached; each climb must be made free from the support or aid of any technology.

Yvon Chouinard, in his 1963 article for the *American Alpine Journal*, proposed that the future of this branch of the climbing tree was not on the cliffs of Yosemite, but upon the remote big walls of the world. It was Jim McCarthy, more frequently than any other climber of that era, who took the additional step and organized and inspired teams to venture onto the seriously remote alpine big walls.

ALMOST ALL OF THE TECHNIQUES used were conceived and perfected in Yosemite Valley, California. The climbs resulting from the application of these techniques were called "Yosemite style" climbs by their first ascentionists. So compelling were the photos and magazine articles these climbers published that it is easy to understand how this new generation completely propogandized the climbing world. Techniques and tactics derided as unacceptable by the generation prior to the Robbins era were acclaimed as the purest style in which to climb by a later generation of enthusiastic converts. It wasn't long before the climbing world adopted not only some of the climbing techniques, but Yosemite ethics and ideals, whether or not these rules suited the shorter cliffs to which they were introduced.

Within each kingdom of climbers, there exist generally held rules that define goals, difficulty, achievement, etc. As time progresses and the difficulty increases, those climbers pushing the standards begin utilizing more and more technology in order to climb more and more difficult walls. This increasingly technical approach often causes the pioneers of the previous generation to shake their heads, and sometimes their fists, in angry disapproval.

Climbers of each succeeding generation rarely appreciate the struggles of their predecessors. They could care less that pioneers had to fight not only gravity, but the prevailing bulwark of a prior generation's ethic.

As each climber and each generation of climbers becomes more and more practiced, they tend to up the ante by omitting certain practices or techniques that only a short time before had been deemed absolutely necessary. Eliminating fixed ropes (a sort of umbilical cord anchored in place as the climbers move upward, ensuring the ability to get back down if the climbers get into trouble) is a good example of upping the ante.

I N 1958, A CLIMBING REVOLUTION occurred when the largest of the Yosemite big walls was first ascended by a team led by Warren Harding. The route, which later became known as The Nose, was begun on July 4, 1957. After many sessions spent climbing, then retreating, going back up to push the high point even higher, then retreating again, The Nose was finished on November 12, 1958. The climbers trailed fixed ropes from bottom to top and placed about 125 bolts along the way. The aid climb was a tremendous breakthrough in what was possible, both technically and psychologically. Moreover, it was a demonstration of what was possible if one had the necessary reserves of tenacity.

Harding's ascent of The Nose was heralded in climbing circles and in the popular press as the magnificent achievement that it was. The Nose was also derided in climbing circles and in the popular press as nothing more than an exercise in endurance and engineering. Soon after Harding's first ascent, Royal Robbins, Tom Frost, Joe Fitschen, and Chuck Pratt repeated The Nose in only six days and without the umbilical cord of fixed ropes. Not long after, the same team (minus

Fitschen) made the first ascent of the Salathé Wall, a great expanse of granite to the left of The Nose. On this climb, the most difficult in the world at the time, fixed ropes were used only for the first one-third of the climb. The progression away from the idea that fixed ropes were necessary had begun.

This illustrates the fact that the elite climbers of each generation are constantly striving to climb harder, or faster, or in "better style" than the climbers of the generation before. They also wish to climb better than their friends did just the week before and, ideally, better than their own efforts only the day before. Climbers are probably as competitive as any group, though the competition manifests itself in camouflaged ways. Climbers name the individual passages they climb up the cliffs and mountains. This is handy not only as a geologic reference, but as a competitive yardstick when relating what one climbed. For example, it is possible to hike to the top of Half Dome. The trail is long and fairly strenuous, and the final several hundred yards follow "the cables." These National Park Service–built cables have been installed by drilling deep holes into the rock and placing hundreds of four-foot-high uprights a sidewalk's width apart. These steel posts hold parallel strands of one-inch-thick cable, and every ten feet or so a wooden plank is laid across the uprights so that a ledge of sorts can be had to stand and to rest. The angle of the slope is indeed impressive, especially to a nonclimber. Thousands of tourists every summer climb up this cable-ladder and upon returning to the valley floor, purchase a T-shirt that proclaims "I Climbed Half Dome." While in one sense they did "climb" Half Dome, theirs is a very different sort of claim from saying "I free climbed The Direct on the NW Face of Half Dome." To imply that one climb is more difficult, more spectacular or more anything is inherently competitive.

Climbers attach very specific ratings with regard to difficulty, length, and style, ostensibly as a means of accurate description. However, the system also lends itself well to being used as either a weapon or as a tool. Often, a climb's "rating" is a rubber knife that is flourished by those skilled enough not

Tom Frost was not only one of America's finest climbers in the 1960s, but he more than any other climber conveyed what it felt like to dangle thousands of feet off the ground. Tom Frost's beautiful black-and-white photos are still among the finest and most inspirational examples of climbing photography. In addition to being a tremendous climber, technical innovator, and photographer, Tom is one of those climbers you always want along with you, especially because he is such a nice guy and a great friend who has a vast supply of the most important ingredient—spirit. Tom once told Paul that one of the greatest moments in his climbing life came during the first ascent of The Salathé; he was aiding into the unknown, out the giant roof, and turned the lip to find himself the first one ever to see the start of the Headwall Crack and to be in one of the most outrageous and beautiful positions in the climbing world.

only to have climbed it, but to have whittled it down to a lower position on a relative scale. It is probably safe to say that by carving away at the difficulty rating, the climber holding the knife hopes that those shavings will pile up and add to his stature. It can get awfully competitive. Climbers tend to deny all of this, since everyone knows climbers disdain competition. One of the things that makes the competition in climbing less overt is that, unlike many other sports, climbing's rules are re-

Falls are commonplace on the most difficult rock climbs,
as the proper sequence of moves is hard to figure out,
as well as being physically demanding.

gional, forever changing and migrating. A basketball player in Slovenia plays by the same rules and regulations as the player in Brooklyn: a shot made or a shot blocked is always just that. If the basketball player in Brooklyn makes a basket from one hundred feet away, it is not from then on considered to be in bad style to have made a basket from under the hoop. However, in climbing the game evolves constantly. This does not in any way denigrate the achievements of the original pioneers.

Todd and I have never been anything less than awed by the achievements of our climbing heroes. Those climbers who, years before us, with vastly inferior and often homemade climbing gear, achieved climbs that in their day were every bit as desperate as the most difficult climbs of today, will forever continue to inspire us. Much of the difficulty in breaking through a barrier in any sport is largely psychological. The burden is always greater for the pioneer, who is in completely new territory and has no yardstick for comparison.

In 1961, when Royal Robbins, Tom Frost, and Chuck Pratt began climbing up the Salathé Wall on El Capitan in Yosemite Valley, they had very definite ideas about the style in which they wished to climb the great rock. Warren Harding and team had adopted a style that allowed fixing ropes the entire length of the climb. In breaking a great psychological barrier, Harding and team had placed about 125 bolts in order to bypass blank sections. Also, in 1957 and '58, wide pitons were unavailable, so when Warren Harding had used all of the wide "pitons" he had crafted from cast-iron stove legs, bolts were drilled in place next to the cracks. By 1961, the experienced Robbins team was aware that it was possible to spend six continuous days on these huge walls. Because of even minor advancements in equipment they could avoid placing as many bolts. The line they had chosen for their new route, the

On well-protected climbs, the fear of falling is much worse than the actual fall. When "going for it," climbers are so focused on upward movement that they are caught by the rope before they completely realize that they have fallen. "Planned falls" are actually much scarier. While photographing this climb, Bill Hatcher said he thought a better photo would result if Paul would "just let go. . . ." This photo is on (or off of) a climb called Cowboy Poetry at the Wild Iris in Wyoming.

Salathé Wall, wasn't nearly as direct as The Nose route. They knew that if piton cracks existed they would be able to follow that line to the top. They knew lots of things from experience. They were confident that these experiences would be the basis for solving new problems en route.

Their burdens were much heavier to bear than those that concern modern-day climbers. Today, we know it is possible to live for long periods of time on such a massive wall. We know the path the route will take, we know that, if we get in trouble and can't self-rescue, an efficient and highly skilled rescue team can pluck us off the wall. In 1961, there wasn't even a thought of a rescue team. All we modern climbers have to do is climb, and our challenge is to contribute further refinements of the game.

Since rock climbing's beginnings, free climbing has been considered the purest style of ascent. When free climbing, the same sort of equipment is used as in aid climbing; however, it is used only for safety and is not used either to rest, or to aid upward progress in any way. Free climbers rely only upon the strength in their hands and their will to hang on. Any use of equipment, no matter how slight, for a rest, support, or to pull upon, instantly transforms the climb into an aid climb. Again, the same ropes and equipment as for aid climbing are used, but only for safety in case of a fall.

When aid climbing came into its glory days, a vocal few derided these newer climbs, such as the Salathé Wall, as "mere engineering feats." In a sense, this criticism was true, but at that time the climbers achieving the climbs were utilizing the only possible means of ascending these walls. Our free ascents were athletically far more difficult, but are psychologically easier in terms of commitment and boldness. Now that we have free climbed these big walls, the game has come full circle, although we too have our detractors. Some say that we should not have used the aid of ropes to help us to learn the "moves" on the difficult pitches. Some detractors tell us that we should have walked to the base, started to climb and, at the first fall, to have come back to the ground.

The aid-climbing pioneers of the 1960s created new techniques and rules to suit their new sport. As they realized that a technique was no longer necessary, they removed it from the rulebook of what was fair within their game. So it is with the free climbing of big walls. Todd and I have improved upon the direct aid style of ascent, which in this day and age has become an anachronism. What once was daring, creative, and technologically the most advanced method of scaling these big walls is, for us, now outmoded. We feel that if climbers truly wish to practice the ethic of constantly improving their style, the time has come to apply the free climbing ethic to the big walls and to treat these long routes as what they are: free climbs.

WHILE WE WERE THE FIRST to free climb the steepest and biggest of North America's big walls, there were several individuals who made groundbreaking free climbs of big walls. Like any endeavor in which advances are made by standing upon the shoulders of giants, Todd and I owe a great deal to the free climbers who, like the aid-climbing pioneers of the 1960s, pointed the way with climbs that continue to inspire us.

Frank Sacherer was a Yosemite free-climbing light burning bright in the 1960s. The stories about Sacherer often revolve around how foolishly bold he could be. In Steve Roper's *Camp 4: Recollections of a Yosemite Rockclimber*, a marvelous account of Roper's Yosemite days, he relates that Layton Kor and other climbers of the time were afraid to climb with Sacherer because of the risks he took, and which he often paid for with very serious and long falls. Nevertheless, he will always be admired for his free ascents of numerous grade IV and V big walls, which include the East and the North Buttresses of Middle Cathedral Rock. In addition, the Northeast Buttress of Higher Cathedral Rock and the Lost Arrow Chimney were long, free contributions. Sacherer's free ascent with Eric Beck in 1965 of the Direct North Buttress of Middle Cathedral Rock (V, 5.10) is today recognized as one of the classic American free climbs.

The highlights of the 1970s were the free ascents of The Regular Route on the Northwest Face of Half Dome (VI, 5.12a) by Jim Erickson, Art Higbee, and Earl Wiggens and the free climb of Astro Man (5.11c), by Ron Kauk, John Bachar, and John Long. The Half Dome climb was marred by the unpleasant nature of the variations that allowed it to be free climbed. It was impressive, however, because it was the first grade VI free climb in North America.

Astro Man is completely unlike Half Dome. The regular North West Face of Half Dome has many wandering pitches of easy-to-moderate climbing. In George Meyers's book *Yosemite Climber*, John Long, one of Astro Man's first free ascentionists, writes:

> The continuous difficulty we had covered was then unheard of; eight out of fourteen leads were 5.10 and several were harder still. Although any technical standard will someday be taken lightly, the positioning of [Astro Man] is truly supreme and beyond all rebuff. All techniques were called into play on a stage of perfect rock and startling exposure. The climbing was classic Yosemite, long blood-pumping cracks up impeccably cleaved dihedrals.

> Astro Man is not only one of the great climbs of Yosemite, but one of the finest in the world. Its classic line and superb climbing, at a widely accessible standard, make it a tremendous experience.

TAKING THE MOST DIFFICULT free climbs of the day as their training apparatus, the talented and dynamic duo of Max Jones and Mark Hudon began the 1980s with extreme free-climbing adventures. These two friends were true explorers. Not only did they strive to pass beyond the frontiers of the possible, but they crossed back over again in order to write about their experiences. This sharing of desire and vision really served to psych me up to try harder on my local crags and to plan realistically to apply my developing skills on dream climbs in other rock arenas.

It is probably fair to say that the most influential and informative English-language climbing magazine of the 1970s and early 1980s was Britain's *Mountain*. This magazine sought to

Todd and Paul were very fortunate to attend the University of Wyoming, as it is near Vedauwoo, a remarkable crack climbing arena in southeast Wyoming. Here they had the best of times climbing and learning a wide variety of techniques that have served them well to this day. In this photo from 1985, Paul is seen during the first ascent of a 5.12d flare problem called New Mutant.

City Park (5.13b/c) was one of the fabled "last great problems" of the thin-crack climbing era. Its allure is a purity of line, a laser-straight, thin slice in a vertical granite wall.

keep its finger on the pulse of what was happening in America and published accounts about Hudon's and Jones's extreme rock climbs and their dreams for the future. My favorite article was "Long, Hard and Free," in which Mark Hudon chronicled the state of affairs of big wall free climbs in America. Excerpted from that article are some of the passages that served to inspire both Todd and me to push our limits at local areas like Vedau-woo, Wyoming, and to begin laying plans for the big wall free climbs of our future:

> To find a free grade V or VI is to find a very rare jewel indeed. Some climbing on walls may never go free. . . . To be free climbing high on El Cap, working out new problems, climbing new free pitches, was almost Nirvana. . . . [Almost] all that was left . . . was the crux aid pitch up to the roof, the roof and the three pitches of the Headwall. Only five pitches, but five pitches of what might turn out to be the most sustained section of rock ever climbed.

> That night while laying in my cot I started to get scared about what I was going to try to free climb the next day. All of the next five pitches made the hardest climbs of my life look like baby routes. It was ridiculous, [above me] was a fifteen foot roof with only three hundred feet of overhanging rock above it and it was only twenty-five hundred feet off the ground, nothing to be scared about! It was ridiculous!

> . . . I know that some of the pitches we free climbed and attempted to free are the most radical climbing ever done on a wall but for some reason I was depressed, bummed out.

> Later, back in the Valley looking at the Headwall through binoculars I noticed the sparrows flying around, darting in and out of the crack. Had we taken the first step towards a new phase of rock climbing?—it didn't bother me anymore because I re-membered that I was once up there flying with those sparrows.

One of the problems with completing the climb was find-ing it in dry conditions. Todd paid a local kid to ride his bike to the base of City Park once a week. The boy was to ascertain the condition of the crack, write "wet" or "dry" on a card, and post it at a nearby store. Todd would call from somewhere "on the road" and ask the store owner to read the note.

The inspiration these two climbers conveyed to Todd and me was immense. Giving our best to climb hard in far-from-Yosemite Wyoming, we often placed ourselves into their stories and found ourselves looking down our own 5.12 pitches and imagining that we were thousands of feet above the treetops.

I had studied and almost worshiped the exploits and achievements of the aid and free climbers who shaped my dreams. I had never met those great climbers who came before, the influences whom Galen Rowell calls "phantom mentors." These teachers weren't there to inspire me in person, but did so by their writings, innovative climbing skills, and belief in their personal vision.

The examples of the integrity and skill of the first climbers to ascend the big walls, as well as the elegant refinements of the free climbers who came later, were taken to heart by Todd and me. Even today I am learning from their contributions, a rich legacy of climbs and evocative writing.

As Todd and I began to add to this legacy, we were honored to receive the sincere congratulations and admiration of history makers. One such example follows:

11/1/88

Paul and Todd,

First of all, Congratulations on free climbing The Salathé! I've waited years for someone with the balls and imagination to go up there and do it. It always bummed me out that the free climbing trend in Yosemite seemed to be moving away from the walls, to shorter and shorter and more useless routes. Max and I would only climb short routes to increase our "flash potential" up on the walls. I used to go around and tell anyone who would listen that anyone with any real ability would be up on the walls free climbing. I really want to get together with you guys and shoot the shit about The Salathé and all the other walls that will go free.

I'm moving to Oregon in January (Hood River to windsurf not Smith Rocks to climb). . . . Please get in touch with me as I want to meet you very much.

Thanks a lot and Congratulations again,
[signed] —Mark Hudon

One of the great innovations in Yosemite climbing occurred when John Salathé (left) invented the hard steel pitons that made possible the long direct-aid climbs in Yosemite and elsewhere. Prior to Salathé's invention, climbers used soft steel pitons, which wore out after only a few placements. This meant that hundreds of pitons would have to be carried on long climbs—which was very impractical. Salathé's pitons could withstand hundreds of placements, allowing climbers to accomplish a great deal by carrying twenty or thirty pitons rather than the weight of several hundred old-style pitons. Salathé's designs were later manufactured, along with many other revolutionary equipment designs by Yvon Chouinard (right). Not only were both men masterful designers, but both are in the pantheon of American climbing heroes. Salathé and Chouinard contributed some of the most significant ascents in North American climbing. It was Chouinard who, after many afternoons spent gazing at El Capitan from the meadow below, eventually pieced together a possible route on the great South West Face of that massive rock, which he named the Salathé Wall in honor of one of his heroes.

It is certain that, prior to the ascent of any of the great direct aid climbs they were to establish, Royal Robbins, Tom Frost, and Chuck Pratt stood transfixed in El Cap meadow and gazed at El Capitan. I can't imagine how exciting it must have been to summon the daring to begin their great unknown adventure up The Salathé. Theirs was the greater boldness, and I envy the thrilling days they shared in friendship climbing this big wall. I envy those golden seasons when the greatest big walls of America were unclimbed or even undreamed of by all but a scant handful of climbers.

Looking through climbers' guidebooks of today, I see photos inscribed with lines showing the paths that aid-climbing routes have taken. On walls like El Capitan, these lines scream with potential for state-of-the-art free climbs.

If the tables were turned and Royal Robbins, Tom Frost, and Chuck Pratt were in El Cap Meadow in 1988, I am certain they would have been the ones who were up on The Salathé struggling, improvising and trying their hardest to make their dream of a free ascent come true. They would have sought out the finest objectives for free climbs on walls both big and small.

THERE IS SOMETHING CAPTIVATING about doing first ascents. It is usually a lot more work, a heck of a lot more uncertain, and, for me, much more rewarding. The pioneering fever I caught from reading Royal Robbins's many accounts of aid climbing adventures on big walls, of Tony Smythe's compelling writing in *Rock Climbers in Action in Snowdonia*, and Chris Bonington's *I Chose To Climb*, as well as stories like Robin Smith's *The Bat and the Wicked*, steeped me in the history and importance of being first. In addition, the photographs that spiced these works were especially powerful influences. The photos taken by John Cleare, Tom Frost, and Galen Rowell seemed more compelling because they were taken on first ascents or early repeats of routes. This is a large part of what causes me to establish new climbs at home and abroad: to gaze up at an El Capitan still beckoning with a new world of free-climbing potential . . . especially the clever combinations of routes which will provide superior, all free linkups in the Heart Route area, as well as The North American Wall and New Jersey Turnpike regions. In the future, the fantastic free climbs on these big walls will not follow aid line–traced photos in guidebooks. Ignoring aid lines, big walls like El Capitan are once again blank spots on the map. New combinations of pitches on these and other gigantic granite canvases will provide great opportunities for outstanding new adventures. These future climbs will stand on their own as the dream-inspiring classics of a new climbing world. Wow! My palms sweat just thinking about being up there in those desperate, thrilling, and yet familiar situations.

We live in a world overflowing with a rich history of great climbers and their inspirational ascents—the same world remains ripe with potential for other climbers to make free-climbing advancements on these gigantic walls. That is, if Todd and I don't get there first!

THE SALATHÉ WALL

VI, 5.13b

AFTER MORE THAN THIRTY days and nights on the Salathé Wall, we were able to read the shadows and tell the hour of the day to the minute. It was 8:45 P.M., and across the valley the Cathedral group had lost its cap of alpenglow. Only an ambient glimmer lit our little world on the wall.

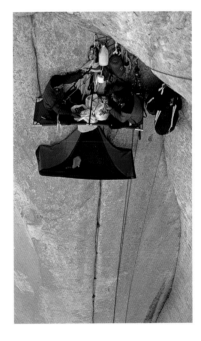

To the casual observer, we might have been the average team aiding toward the security of a bivvy on Long Ledge. But as Todd neared the belay his movements became less fluid, his confident swimming motions from jam to jam turning stiff and choppy. In the growing darkness, I thought I could see his forearms glowing. Arms pumped to the point of fusion provided enough light to see, but Todd couldn't crank the last few moves or even swear during the inevitable thirty-foot plummet. Dejected, he slumped at the end of the rope, then swung back into the rock.

El Capitan reflected in the Merced River. The Nose route is the line between light and shadow, while The Salathé begins near The Nose and meanders up to the heart-shaped depression. From near The Heart's left side, The Salathé route heads more or less straight to the top of the wall.

We hung on the belay anchors, sapped. The ground was some 3,000 feet below, and here we were, perched in the middle of an overhanging sweep of granite. We pulled the rope and slid down into a darkness as black as our fatigue and as daunting as the herculean task we had begun. Our porta-ledge camp under the Great Roof was a secure hang, but tonight it was not a home. The Salathé's headwall remained taunting and smug in its glorious position.

People had been climbing big walls in Yosemite for several years, but the first ascent of the Salathé Wall in 1961 was a real breakthrough. The year before, Joe Fitschen, Tom Frost, Chuck Pratt, and Royal Robbins had made the second ascent of The Nose in six days without the use of fixed ropes; it was the first time a major El Capitan route had been done in a single continuous push, but this adventurous climb was just a precursor of what was to come.

Frost, Pratt, and Robbins had an even more ambitious plan: their proposed Salathé Wall would link a series of cracks with far fewer bolts than the 125 that The Nose had required. After fixing the first third of the route, the trio dropped their ropes and pushed on to the upper 2,000 feet of vertical to the overhanging wall. At the end of the sixth day, they topped out, having used just thirteen bolts for the entire route.

At that time, the Salathé Wall was the state of the art in technical difficulty. This supremely talented and bold team created pitches, both free and aid, that were as difficult as anything that had been done previously. If they blew it, they would have had to rely on themselves alone for a rescue. In 1961, being 2,000 feet up a Yosemite wall was a lot farther off the deck than it is today.

In many ways, it is logical to use aid on a big wall. The prospect of falls, or of trying to keep it together on a very thin crux way off the ground, seemed too frightening to consider. But for Todd Skinner and me, free climbing high up on a big wall was the stuff dreams are made of.

For us, this dream was brought to life by an article in *Mountain* (May/June 1981, no. 79). In "Long, Hard and Free," Mark Hudon and Max Jones described their free-climbing efforts on the big walls of Yosemite. We marveled at their audacity and boldness, and began to think that it was possible for us to climb long, hard, and free as well. Soon, the Salathé Wall, the "greatest rock climb in the world," was lodged in our minds.

Todd spent the spring of 1985 in Yosemite, and this was the practical beginning of our quest. After completing the first free ascent of The Stigma, Todd phoned, but I was unconvinced

Easily one of the most dramatic camping spots in the world, this bivouac atop El Cap Spire was not conducive to long midnight strolls. Todd is seen beginning the day's work by leading a 5.11c fingercrack.

and remained in Laramie. Not yet dismayed, he packed five days' supply of food, gathered a team, and assumed The Salathé was his.

According to Todd, they were lucky to aid the route, much less free climb it, but what he saw inspired another look. A year later his second reconnaissance encountered a similar fate, and he was stopped again by the pendulum to Hollow Flake. The team didn't search for an alternative, but free climbed the pitches that went easily and quickly, aiding those that would be the cruxes that he and I encountered in 1988.

At about the 1,000-foot level, Paul is experiencing the climb's first relatively difficult pitch (5.12b), a variation called Stefan's Traverse (in honor of Stefan Glowacz, the first to solve this climbing puzzle during his attempt to free The Salathé), which eliminates the pendulum to the Hollow Flake.

Curiously enough, on both attempts, the teams were so inexperienced at aid climbing and so terribly slow that they often encountered the pitches they most wanted to case well after dark. So, after a total of about ten days on the route, Todd was only a little more convinced of the feasibility of freeing The Salathé. Even though there were sections of the climb that he hadn't looked at with an eye toward free climbing, the vibes felt right. Todd was confident that a free line could be found somewhere on the face.

Within a few days of this last reconnaissance, Todd and I were scheming in Boulder, Colorado, frantically drawing topos, examining photos of the wall, and looking for free-climbing options on adjacent routes. Fearful of rival teams, we allowed no one to sit in on these planning sessions—not even girlfriends. The knowledge was committed to memory, and the topos we drew were shredded and burned. The ashes were mailed to parts of the world where English isn't spoken. To the outside world, we hoped it would appear that The Salathé was not free climbable. Since neither of us owned watches, we synchronized our calendars. A pact was made: we would be in the Valley by May 1, and we would gamble our health, our esteem in the eyes of our families, and what little wealth we could command to arrive on time at the gate of dreams.

The ensuing months were spent in the gym, utilizing a secret training system devised from all we could learn from the French and Soviet climbers. Endless mornings on the boulders fed our desires. As our strength increased, so did our phone bills. But the long-distance psyche sessions between Hueco Tanks, Texas, and Boulder made possible many more lat pulls and forced one more lap on the bouldering circuit. "The Winter is long—yet the robin has a song to sing," says the proverb. While we weren't too concerned about singing on key, we wanted to be able to sing loud.

We learned from the grapevine that Stefan Glowacz had joined a little-known fraternity of Europeans, including Heinz Mariacher and Manolo, who had tried to free The Salathé. After ten days of effort, he had come away with the prediction

The Free Salathé Wall

FA 1961 by Royal Robbins,
Tom Frost, Chuck Pratt.
"The Greatest Rock Climb in the World"
FFA June 1988 by Todd Skinner
and Paul Piana.

Topo labels (top to bottom, right side and center):

- (13) Lung Ledge 4th class
- (12)
- 5.10b
- 5.11d x
- 5.8 (11) Heart Ledges
- Mammoth Terraces (10)
- 165'
- down climb
- 5.10b
- 5.7
- (8)
- 5.8 chimney
- Half Dollar
- 5.10b
- (7)
- (6)
- El Cap Spire (21)
- 5.6 chimney
- The Alcove bivvy
- (20) 5.10a
- 5.13b
- 5.10d fist
- many bad bolts, bashies
- 5.11b
- (5)
- 5.10b
- 5.10d
- (4)
- 5.10b
- (3)
- 5.7
- (19) The Ear scariest 5.7 in the world!
- (18) 5.10d/.11a
- (17) 5.10a
- (16) 5.9
- 5.7 chimney
- Hollow Flake Ledge bivvy (15)
- (2)
- 5.11b
- 5.8
- (1)
- 5.10c
- 5.11a (13) Stephan's traverse
- 25' Horizontal
- 5.12a
- The Roof
- (29)
- 5.12b/c 1b poor pro
- (28) x
- 5.11d 1b
- Sous la Toit Ledge (tiny) (27)
- 5.10b
- 5.11d
- Scramble
- outline of rock that fell
- (36)
- 5.9
- chinese puzzle rock
- 5.11a (35)
- Fan 5.10d/.11a hands
- (34)
- (26) sloping bivvy
- The Block
- (25) wet!
- 5.10c
- (24)
- 5.12d x Teflon Corner
- 5.11a overhanging knobs (33) Long Ledge bivvy
- 5.13b pod
- 5.12c fingers
- (32)
- 5.13c enduro
- Lactic Eclipse pitch
- (31) x
- Vedauwoo flare pitch
- 5.13a
- (30)
- 5.12a super thrilling
- (29)
- (23)
- 5.10d
- 5.11a
- (22)
- 5.9 squeeze
- 5.11c finger stacks
- pod
- El Cap Spire
- belay high or do 175 ft pitch
- 5.9 ow
- (14)
- 5.12b

that it would not go. Several pitches could not be bypassed, and, according to Stefan, the pitch above the Great Roof, if it could be done at all, would resist attempts for at least ten years.

While at the competitions in Europe in 1987, Todd tried to get as much beta, or detail, out of Stefan as possible without giving away our plans. What we learned was disheartening, and we suspected that he too was "playing the game." But we were happy to discover that he had found a way to bypass the pendulum to Hollow Flake, via a 5.12b traverse sixty feet lower.

In much the same way that a driver refers to an auto map, rock climbers utilize topographic maps of the routes charted up cliff faces. These "topos" provide similar traveler's information: lengths between rest stops (bivouacs), type of road surface ahead (finger crack, off-width, etc.) difficulty of the terrain (5.10b, 5.13a etc.), and colorful place names.

OUR ARRIVAL IN YOSEMITE was almost not to be. On May Day, racing north from Hueco Tanks, Todd blew an engine in Raton, New Mexico. He broke the news to me in a midnight call. We were screwed—my bus hadn't run in five months. With help from his brother Orion, Todd arrived, only a day later, in Boulder. Miraculously, my bus started, and we traded a dead horse for a dying one and rode north into Wyoming.

The spring blizzards waited until our ailing bus tottered across the howling, windswept eternity of I-80. The geriatric VW could manage 40 m.p.h. downhill and got eight miles to the gallon. At every gas stop, and there were many, the starter refused to work, so each time I had to go underneath with a screwdriver to short the connection. As if deep slush, mud, and cold weren't enough, ten minutes were spent at each stop chipping away the massive accumulations of ice in order to reach the starter.

We arrived in Pinedale, Wyoming, Todd's hometown, at 3 a.m. in a second-gear headwind and slept fitfully, dreaming that the bus would never start again. In the morning, after a quick overhaul, we had a vehicle that raced along at 50 m.p.h. and got a stunning twelve miles to the gallon. On the road again.

We finally arrived in Yosemite, knowing that we wouldn't be able to just walk up and climb the route free. It would involve an unheard-of amount of continuously difficult climbing, and from Todd's recon efforts and those of others, it was

obvious that The Salathé couldn't be touched without a lot of preparation.

We decided that a series of "camping trips" would allow us to gain the necessary knowledge and to become accustomed to life so far off the ground. Our strategy was to spend six or seven days at a time working on different sections of the wall. These trips were also used to cache water and the occasional can of beans at critical sites. During this stage we often camped in the Alcove, the large and comfortable ledge at the base of El Cap Spire. We preferred its sheltered nature to the more famous and aesthetic bivouac on El Cap Spire. This also allowed other parties the unique experience of sleeping on top of the spire.

After our work low on the route—that is, up to pitch 24—it became difficult to haul enough water and food to points higher on the wall. Our tactics changed and we drove to Tamarack Flat Campground. The entrance was locked at the highway, so we began our hike to the top of El Capitan from there, carrying huge loads of food, ropes, and gear over almost twelve miles of very hilly trail.

Near the summit, we located a nice spot for our recon camp and began outrageous rappels off the rim. I couldn't help but laugh at the ridiculous nature of rappelling down El

A tremendous amount of matériel is necessary to climb big walls. Critical omissions from this array are several Edgar Rice Burroughs "Martian Stories" novels; A Man Called Noon *by Louis L'Amour, and* A Raymond Chandler Omnibus, *as well as Pop Tarts, Super Glue, tortillas, and tuna.*

Capitan. What had seemed like hideous exposure on pitch 24 suddenly seemed no worse than the void experienced on short free climbs. We went as far as Sous le Toit ledge, leaving fixed ropes that were ultimately anchored to a big block just over the rim. We then climbed back out to a stance just at the lip of the Great Roof and began work on the crack in the Headwall.

Several days were spent on these headwall pitches as we top-roped or led them, or sussed out the protection, and just got used to being in such an exposed place. We were continually impressed by the boldness of Frost, Pratt, and Robbins, who had dared to risk it all and were there first in 1961.

Todd and I marveled that at each impasse there was a sequence that worked, even if just barely, yet we were appalled by the inhuman amount of difficult climbing. Both of us were haunted by the specter of injury. Damage to a critical joint or tendon would finish our bid. A turn in the weather could be equally demoralizing. Occasionally the mental strain of so many difficult sequences and unrelenting crux pitches became a burden that threatened to crush our dream.

EVERY WORKING DAY ON the headwall ended in a multipitch jug to the rim and a joyous campfire at our summit camp. One of the most enjoyable nights was spent with a group of Kiwis who had topped out late in the day and had brought along a celebratory bag of marshmallows. Toasting marshmallows on the summit of El Capitan with good friends is a night I'll long remember.

We were chased off the summit twice—once by snow and once when we ran out of food. The latter posed a serious problem, as we were also out of money. I had survived the past two weeks on 47 cents, and Todd was the rich man of the team with twelve bucks still in his pocket.

We really needed to perfect the pitch that exits the Headwall onto Long Ledge. During our recons, this area had been a bottleneck as we sat on Long Ledge waiting for parties to aid climb past. We desperately needed another camping trip to figure out this pitch, but hadn't the greenbacks to spend on even another day on the wall. However, we knew we would stay no matter how hungry we became, and often commented on how trusting the deer were in Yosemite.

To fund our Salathé quest we had a yard sale in the Camp IV parking lot. We auctioned everything we thought we could live without: a brand new pair of rock shoes, climbing slippers, Friends and carabiners, virtually everything except our souls. Each sale saw our feed bag swelling not just with beans and tortillas, but with treats that would keep our morale high. Pop Tarts were morning essentials, and Snickers and raisins were great for lunch. Eventually we had enough cash to fund either another recon or a final push, but not for both. We chose the latter, as there was little else we could sell. We knew we had a good chance of pulling it off if we could stay together physically and if the weather stayed cool and dry.

We brought four extra cans of tuna in case we had to spend four extra days on the wall. Photographer Bill Hatcher and our "Wall Master," Scotsman John Christie, would climb just ahead of us. The plan was for John to lead, allowing Bill to lower back down to take photos of Todd and me. From the Block, John and Bill would punch it to the top. Then Bill would fix ropes back down for photos, while John would go down the East ledges, thus sparing precious rations.

The route had been steadily whittling away at our fingers and we knew this might make the difference between success and failure. We also felt that we'd need a rest day up high, but were concerned that the weather might not allow one. We were very fortunate to find that "Mad Dog" Bob Boehringer, a veteran of Todd's 1985 recon, was in the Valley. We recruited Bob, this time as Radio Free Salathé, and every evening at 9:30 we would receive a current weather report.

Armed with a month of reconnaissance, food and water, radio support, and a super photo team, our final push was ready to get off the ground and onto the Big Stone. We had done our homework, but the magnitude of the final fight was still a heavy burden. Yet without the burden there would be no appeal. We looked upward and vowed to take no prisoners.

THE SALATHÉ BEGINS WITH ten pitches known as the Free Blast. The first three are wonderful, but the fourth and fifth are so trashed out that we were ashamed they were in America. The wall is pasted with huge, useless, saucer-sized blobs of aluminum that have been beaten into old bolt holes. Faded and tattered runners hang from everything, and the belays are of the same poor quality. The Free Blast could be repaired and become the quality climb it once was, but until that happens it remains an embarrassment to the supposed ethic that hypocritical American climbers care about preserving the rock, the experience, and our image.

A relic from climbers who had passed this way before. This rusty old piton is one of many we encountered along the way.

After the Free Blast and a 5.10a downclimb to Heart Ledge, we were happy to climb Stefan's traverse to Hollow Flake. After this desperate pitch, the infamous Hollow Flake must be dealt with, and I was horrified to learn that a 50-meter rope isn't long enough to enable the leader to reach the top of the flake. Todd struggled higher and higher on this completely unprotected pitch as I quickly untied the belay and simul-climbed with him. I figured that only one of us needed to be freaked out, so I neglected to mention this to Todd until I had reached the top of the flake.

Our original plan called for avoiding the aid pitch above the ear by climbing an offwidth crack just to the left. Steve Schneider had run these 5.10d pitches out during the first ascent of Bermuda Dunes, but we both doubted our offwidth skills and wanted nothing to do with such a loathsome technique. Since we were aesthetically repulsed by this vile crevice, we decided we would have our way with the original aid pitch or else abandon the climb.

The 5.13b pitch turned out to be a beauty. Were it on the ground, this tight dihedral would be a much-tried classic, but the 1,500-foot approach will deter many. This was the first crux

"This 5.13b pitch turned out to be a beauty."
Todd's vast experience gained by establishing some of the
world's most difficult thin-crack test pieces was of
tremendous value on this particular rope length.

and it required a wide variety of crack techniques. We found power flares, 5.12+ dynos from them into pin scars and back out again, thuggish laybacking—and then we found the crux. Searing, fingertip pin scars, laser precise edging, and post-doctoral skills in body English were the ingredients of the last twenty feet of this pitch.

Two rope lengths above El Cap Spire we reached an impasse at an A1 pitch. Several days had been spent here on our reconnaissance trying to find something that worked. While the first half went relatively easily at 5.12a, the second half resisted everything we threw at it.

We had spent days trying to top-rope three possible variations to the right. Faces that looked as though we would have them at a glance slapped us around as though we were a pair of Raymond Chandler's dumb blondes. We would try one and get slapped. We would try another and get slapped. We were tired of being slapped.

We left the pretty faces for a glassy open book to the left. It looked impossibly smooth so we put the moves on the arete in between. Todd soon found it was smoother than our moves. I lowered down and tried all my best lines. The smoothest refusal we had ever received met me in that corner, and I was overjoyed that on the final push, Todd won the 5.12d pitch with powerful stemming, several more-than-playful slaps, and no falls.

And then it was on to the Block, a perfectly situated but hideously sloping balcony from which we could lounge in relative comfort and gaze at the sweeping perfection of the Headwall. The ropelength below the Block was the bad neighborhood of The Salathé, a slummy pitch hung with moss tendrils and streaming with water. It is as ugly as the Headwall is beautiful—as if someone had diverted a sewer through the

We were thrilled with the pitch due to its savage technical challenge, and happy that it came at the 1,400-foot level—when we were fresh, early on in the climb, as it turned out to be the most difficult of the 5.13 pitches on the Free Salathé.

Louvre. Climbing it was not a pretty sight, and invective flowed as freely as the mud in the jams.

Once on the Block things got better. The rock above was dry and clean. The bivvy on this sloped perch was the last grand floor to walk around upon; we could drop gear and get it back. Here we spread out the picnic and glopped stolen Degnan's condiments on bean-smeared "Manna from Hell," the petrified, jerky-like tortillas Todd learned to make from an ancient Mexican woman. We ate until we were full, or until our

jaws were cramped from chewing. We paced in little circles. We dropped things just to see them stop falling. We slept.

The morning saw us moving toward the Great Roof. The pitches were increasingly difficult—a portent of ropelengths to come. The pitch below the Great Roof was especially memorable. Powerful, open-handed laybacking and technically desperate stemming was protected by horribly frayed bashies and an unwillingness to fall. Our aching backs called this flaring dihedral 5.12b.

Worn by eons of rain-water, this open book–like groove which we called The Teflon Corner is shiny smooth. It looked so impossibly slick that we spent several days trying other alternatives before attempting this marble-polished option. In this photo, Todd is seen nearing the end of the glassy crux.

The pitch ended at a dangling stance below the amazing Great Roof. This bold feature stair steps over and out for twenty feet and with the walls of the corner below, cocooned us from the wind. We hauled our bags and set up our porta-ledge camp.

THE FIRST NIGHT OF SEVERAL WAS spent here, lives and gear tangled across the hanging corner like some giant cobweb. Our little world was quite secure, but we could never truly relax: the position was too spectacular. Dropped gear fell a long, long way before we lost sight of it.

We had to be careful to keep everything tied in and only failed this test once. Todd and I had taken as many Louis L'Amour novels as we could scrounge. We had finished the batch and had pored through the Edgar Rice Burroughs *Martian Stories* as well. Todd was well into *Thuvia, Maid of Mars*, but I was left with a romance novel that Bill Hatcher had fought through, complaining with every page. It accidentally slipped from my ledge and became the fastest read of the climb. I started rereading *Hondo*.

The next morning I awakened slowly—I must have been dreaming of Mars. As the sky brightened, I thought I heard the faintest clash of sword on sword. I peeked cautiously over the edge of the suspended cot and glimpsed Todd, still asleep, scything and parrying with some dream-induced, green-skinned Martian warrior. On his face was a confident fighting smile.

The next pitch was a stiff cup of coffee. From the top floor of our camp, the route moved out right with lots of cool morning beneath our heels, an easy but spectacular traverse leading to an attention-getting series of deadpoint surges to sloping buckets. From here it is possible to brachiate wildly to the right, feet swinging, and then to throw your leg up over a huge horizontal spike in the same way a L'Amour hero would mount a galloping horse.

What a place! Halfway out a huge roof, a hundred miles off the deck, is an amazing saddlelike peninsula so flat and

"The first night of several was spent here, lives and gear tangled across the hanging corner like some giant cobweb. Our little world was quite secure, but we could never truly relax, the position was too spectacular. Dropped gear fell a long, long way before we lost sight of it."

Hanging camp below the Great Roof.

"This pitch was a stiff cup of coffee. From the top floor of our camp, the route moved out right with lots of cool morning beneath our heels. Had I fallen, I surely would have screamed." The photo shows Paul at the lip of the Great Roof (5.12a), twenty horizontal feet out from camp and almost 3,000 above the treetops. Paul says, *"When you look down from this point it takes five minutes to see the ground!"*

comfortable that we could have served coffee on it—not that it was still required.

From the saddle, it's all rounded buckets to the lip and a terrifying heel-toe above the head and crank to a shoulder scum where, had I fallen, I surely would have screamed. All the while my heart was slugging away, doing Mike Tyson imitations while I made the tenuous step up onto a hands-down rest. We decided to throw in a belay here since we had the stance.

Stefan Glowacz had told Todd that he didn't think the pitch above the Great Roof would ever go, but, fortunately, years of climbing Vedauwoo's flares served us well. From the belay it looked pretty grim. Scarred by pitons and scabbed over with useless lumps of ruined bashies and one sad fixed piton, this short pitch was one to be feared.

The first 5.12+ flare moves were harder than any I had ever experienced and were unprotected as well. How the jams felt meant nothing—they were so bad that Todd had to visually monitor his hand throughout each move. With his climbing shoes 15 unprotected feet above the belay he had to pull up slack to clip a tied off peg. So flaring were the jams that it was impossible to downclimb and the slightest error, even a change in the blood pressure in Todd's hand, would see The Salathé flick him off and would send him screaming far below the roof, until the force of the fall would crash onto my belay anchors with Todd wide-eyed and spinning thousands of feet off the ground.

We were both glad that he didn't fall. The flares ended with a thankfully short but tremendously difficult face sequence. Power, grace, tremendous skill, and the essence of boldness were some of the practices Todd pulled from our bag of tricks. We were ecstatic that the second 5.13 pitch was done, but sobered because two more were just above.

The Headwall must be the grandest climb in the universe, a beautiful and inspiring crack system splitting the 100-degree sweep of the golden wall at the top of El Capitan. The essence of The Salathé is distilled in this one incredible fissure. To be here, whether free climbing or aiding, is one of the most overwhelmingly good experiences a rock climber can have.

"So flaring were the hand jams that the slightest error would see The Salathé flick him off and would send him screaming far below the roof, until the force of the fall would crash onto my belay anchors, with Todd wide-eyed and spinning thousands of feet off the ground." In this photo, Todd is shown climbing this serious first Headwall pitch 5.13a. The addition of a bolted belay and especially a protection bolt by an unknown (to us) later party have lessened the psychological difficulty, as well as making the crux easier by allowing the use of a formerly occupied piton scar to climb higher in the flared crack before traversing to the main Headwall Crack.

It is indeed a beauty, one that cannot be wooed with mere technique, but a prize to be fought for. Todd and I feared the unrelenting pump of this pitch. The Headwall Crack became the object of Todd's desire. He wanted to free "the most beautiful crack I've ever seen," in the most impressive position either of us could imagine.

This day it was not to be. Todd gave it his best, failing twice just a move away from the anchor. In the last of the day's light, I thought he had it when his foot rocketed off the wall as a little flake snapped. He fell thirty feet, too flamed to even curse. He hung a few moments, toes brushing the wall, then I belayed him to his highest piece so that he could unclip and downjump far enough to be lowered to the belay.

Against all hope, Todd went up again, but even ten feet off the belay, it was obvious that he was too tired to succeed. Still he gave his best. Violent karate chop jamming, frantic foot changes, and missed clips, then at ninety feet out, a dejected murmur in the gloom—I was yanked upward and into the wall as Todd hit the end of the rope.

Rappelling over the roof in the darkness was scary. We would get to the bottom of the fixed loop and yard ourselves into the hanging camp. The valley was dark, the highway a thin stream of yellow light as cars flowed into Yosemite. Dinner was a quiet affair. At that moment we felt like we were too far off the ground, the gloom altogether too black. The night was long.

THE HALF-LIGHT OF DAWN was the same monochrome gray as the ceiling above, and I might have been staring at it for hours when Todd announced that he was still really beat and needed a rest day.

By this time, we both could have used a rest week. Neither of us could close our hands,

At the end of each pitch, Todd and Paul would anchor themselves to the cliff, hanging from equipment placed in the rock. Especially thousands of feet off the deck, it is important to keep the system orderly so that at a glance a climber can see that he is safely clipped in.

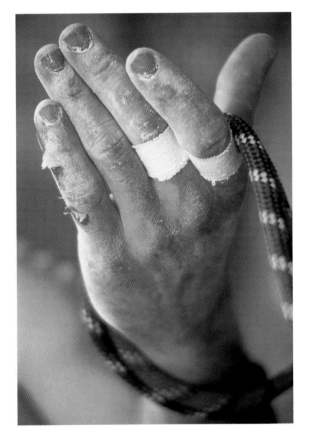

High on the wall during our final push, we couldn't afford to take time off so that our shredded fingers could heal, so we would squirt Super Glue into the wound, pinch it shut and then add a wrap of athletic tape. Good as new, almost! Cuts were easy to repair, but pressure gouges and scrapes—called "gobies" in climber slang—were problematic, as they would ooze through Super Glue and tape, thereby lubricating the finger and hand jams.

and our critical forefingers had been brutally bludgeoned by the many cruel pin-scars. Our knuckles were swollen to a shocking size. We were concerned that we would tear ourselves apart before we could finish, but with our limited rations, taking the time to rest and to heal wasn't a game we could afford to play.

By this time, Bill and John had topped out, and Bill had fixed lines back down to take photos. Rather than waste a day resting, we decided that we would jumar their ropes to the pitch that exited onto Long Ledge. I had been having better success on it than Todd, so we figured that I should work it some more and then Todd could still have the Headwall Crack.

We spent a frustrating day on this exit crack. I could almost do it, but would fail a few feet short every time. I must have fallen a nautical mile that day, but we gained valuable knowledge about subtle foot placements, and Todd did get a little rest. Even so, I was afraid I wouldn't be able to do it at all. After hours of failure, my severely gobied fingers would ooze quickly through Super Glue and tape, so we retreated to our hanging camp and worked at repairing my fingers.

It was my night to be depressed. I tried to relax and sleep but couldn't. I climbed that pitch a thousand times in my mind. Todd slept deeply, dreaming once more of defending the honor of the most beautiful Martian woman, swords glinting in the sun.

MORNING BROUGHT APPREHENSION and a slow stalling breakfast. Having put it off long enough, we started up the fixed lines to do battle with the Headwall. Todd clipped his ascenders onto the thin, red arc that swooped out and disappeared over the lip.

From his spectacular dangle he looked back just as I was "buried at sea." This was the term we used to describe the

In a view down the hundred-degree, overhanging Headwall, Todd is shown climbing what he described as "the most beautiful crack I've ever seen." Paul remembers that they were especially fatigued after almost thirty days on this climb, and Todd began referring to this forearm-burning stretch of the wall as The Lactic Eclipse.

Far above the valley floor and nearing the top of the Salathé Wall, Paul is leading the last part of the Headwall Crack (5.13b). Even though climbing equipment is as reliably strong 3,000 feet off the ground as it is only a hundred feet up, there are moments when one's emotions are overwhelming and this fact is of little comfort.

frightening and amusing fall one took when unbalancing a porta-ledge. I had weighted the ledge a little too close to one end and dramatically slid off and fell to the end of my tether. Todd's laughter faded over the lip and after calming down I joined him at the start of his pitch.

Todd felt a bit hesitant so early in the morning and needed to clear his mind. He climbed fifteen and then twenty feet above the piece he hung from and dramatically hurled himself into the void. He repeated this six or seven times, until it became fun and the reluctance to go for it was completely gone.

Back at the belay we looked down at the still-dark valley floor. The sun hadn't hit the face, and the winds of the Headwall were still. Todd flowed through the stillness and all the difficulties, slowing at the last few moves, taking care to make no mistakes. And then all the fears we had for this pitch turned to laughter as he clipped the belay and I started up to join him.

I was happy that the beauty had been won, but afraid of what was just above. Todd and I spent at least an hour cleaning my hands with alcohol, super-glueing the rents in my fingers, and then carefully applying a wrap of tape over the glue. Before starting, I torqued my fingers in the crack to numb the pain.

The morning's lethargy became adrenalin as the thin jams were suddenly below and I found myself wedged into a podlike slot. Exiting the slot seemed particularly rude to my tattered hands, its flared jams as painful as backhanding a wire brush. After clipping the highest piece, I lost my nerve and decided to downclimb into the pod to rest. I was afraid to fall again.

The fear wasn't the usual fear of falling—the gear was good and we had lived so long up here that the drop was not the rope-clenching horror it had been more than thirty days before. My phobia was failure. I couldn't bear the agony without succeeding on this pitch. I fell while downclimbing.

The next try was as solid as could be. The pitch seemed to flow together until I found myself staring at the dyno target. Todd was screaming "Hit it! Hit it! Hit it!" Long seconds passed while I pondered failure, either from missing the dyno or from a lack of trying. A deliberate lunge and I pinched the knob so hard that Arnold Schwarzenegger would have been proud. I cranked to the belay, laughing and waving my arms like a lunatic.

WE SPENT THE REST of the day rappelling back down to the camp under the Great Roof and packing our gear. We slowly hauled it up to Long Ledge and enjoyed walking back and forth. It was late, but we yearned for the prize, so, leaving the haul bags, we climbed for the top.

Rising above the left end of Long Ledge is a face climbing extension of the Headwall. The variation pitch we established up this overhanging knobby wall was one of our favorite parts of the climb. In the photo of this 5.12a pitch, Todd is seen powering up this billowing sheet of granite on rounded hand holds.

Todd and Paul are seen just two rope lengths below the summit. The end of their quest and almost certain success lights their faces with smiles that erase the weeks of long, hard work of free climbing this majestic wall.

The next pitch is one of the gems of the climb. From the extreme left edge of Long Ledge an overhanging, knobby wall rolls and bulges upward. Todd reveled in the delicate foot changes, long reaches between knobs, and deadpoints to crisp side pulls. After he had danced up this 5.12a Hueco-esque wonder, I enjoyed a superb 5.10 thin hand crack which put us only one pitch from the top. Todd made light work of the last bit of 5.11, and the Free Salathé was done.

Our long, hard work had nearly ended and we were indescribably happy as we raced the sunset back down to Long Ledge to radio John Christie and our other friends in the meadow that The Salathé was ours! We spent the most satisfying bivvy of our lives eating extra Pop Tarts, drinking lots of water, singing funny songs, and discussing the finer quotes from Louis L'Amour. Tomorrow would be a grand celebration!

THE NEXT MORNING WAS PERFECT. We breakfasted and started hauling freight to the rim. We joked about being extra careful, as most fatal auto accidents are said to occur within two miles of home. I was the first over the rim and selected the best anchor I could find. We had already used this huge block, as had years of Salathé climbers.

Off to one side was a fixed piton to which I anchored Todd's line. I plugged in a #1 Friend to make sure. While Todd ascended the pitch I used the block as a hauling anchor and as my tie-in as well. When the bags reached the lip, I was unable to pull them over myself, and waited for Todd to arrive.

While waiting, I decided that I might as well be embarrassingly paranoid and clip the fixed pin as well. Todd reached the rim and I made him pose for pictures like Layton Kor at the

top of The Salathé. Since he was on top and pulling up an extra rope, I began taking out the anchors. I removed the Friend, then turned and started lifting the haul bags. We heard a terrible grating noise and, turning back, were horrified to see that somehow the block had come loose!

I'm not exactly clear about what happened next. Todd remembers me putting my hands out at the block and yelling "No!" I do remember the two of us being battered together, and the horror of seeing my best friend knocked wildly off the edge, and then a tremendous weight on my left leg as I was squeegied off the rim. I recall a loud crack like a rifle shot, then more pummeling, and suddenly everything stopped spinning and I could just peek back up over the edge.

Everything was in tatters, ropes pinched off and fused—it appeared that they had all been cut. I was afraid to touch anything, and sick with the knowldege that Todd had probably just hit the talus. Suddenly, a startling bass squeak sounded below me, followed by a desperate "Grab the rope!"

I hauled myself over the top, and soon a bloody hand on a

The Salathé Wall, Free at Last! Todd is pictured at the very rim of the great Salathé Wall. Moments later, disaster struck when the huge block used as the team's penultimate anchor came loose, crushing them and dragging them back over the edge. Paul and Todd were saved by—and for a while were dangling from—a single, damaged strand of a climbing rope which Paul, as an afterthought, had clipped into an ancient, poorly driven piton.

A photo of the tattered remains of the climbing rope that saved our bacon. This was returned to us by the Yosemite Search and Rescue Team who, the next day, policed up the scattered wreckage. Our haul bags full of equipment, along with the massive rock that had been our anchor, fell the full height of the wall and exploded into the talus. A couple of carabiners and the stems of several Friends were bent into V-shapes, and a shoe was torn almost in half at the instep. We had a stuff sack that held a can of tuna, a bag of M&M's, and a 3-oz. bottle of Super Glue; apparently this vaporized on impact, and to this day some of my climbing gear reclaimed from the wreck has bits of candy and fish glued to it. The compact Rollei camera that Bill Hatcher had lent us (and which was used to take the photos on pages 65 and 68) was clipped to the loop of rope that had been tied to the huge block that came loose. Those two photos were the little camera's last. Amazingly, it did not pop open and the pictures were okay. Todd and I were happy to take a more circuitous route, literally crawling down from the summit of El Capitan.

crushed ascender slid over the rim. I helped Todd up and we laid there for a long time. We were terrified because Todd was having trouble breathing and his pelvic area hurt very badly. My leg was in a really weird position and reaching a crescendo of pain.

I don't know how long we were there, afraid to move for fear of fainting and unraveling the braid of cut ropes that held us. When we did get up we discovered that Todd's line appeared to be okay. He had been held by one of his CMI ascenders. Apparently, the rock had scraped over the ascender and, miraculously, that small, gouged and bent piece of metal had kept Todd's rope from being cut. I had been held by the loop I'd clipped to the fixed pin. The 11mm rope with which I had tied into the block had been cut as easily as a cotton shoelace. Two other 9mm ropes were in eight or nine pieces, and the haul bags were talus food.

We coiled the remaining rope and slowly started down the East Ledges. A descent that usually took us just under two hours required almost seven, and we arrived at the base of Manure Pile Buttress looking much worse than the average wall climber who staggers down that trail. Besides being battered, cut, and more than a little rattled, Todd suffered several broken ribs, and a piece of bone was broken off of his hip bone. My left leg was severely gouged and broken in five places.

W E HAD DREAMED, we had trained, and we had struggled. Even though the climb ended with a nightmare, we had triumphed. I'm sure that the ecstasy will live inside us forever.

Sometimes at night, as I'm drifting off to sleep, I suddenly hear that big block move and I see Todd tumble off the rim. I think about how difficult it would have been for our families if we had been killed. I shudder at the remembrance of being dragged off the summit of El Capitan and knowing that we really were going to die. For me, the definition of "horror" is now an emotion.

Now that years have passed, and Todd and I have healed, I'm even more pleased with our climb. Especially for 1988, the climbing is unrelenting in its severity and the logistics are staggering. We worked harder than anyone else was willing to work, harder than we thought we could. We were willing to see our most shining goal become a tormenting failure. Yet we were prepared to fail and fail and fail until we finally could succeed.

We are very happy and very proud of having made the first free ascent of The Salathé; not just because of perseverance and success but because it proved that great work yields great reward. I'm pleased that by opening this milestone of a door, we had learned to walk bravely through—to continue in our quest to live out our wildest dreams.

SALATHÉ POSTSCRIPT

T HINKING BACK ON THE First Free Ascent of The Salathé, I enjoy reliving the great days on that majestic wall. Days full of harsh labor, spectacularly exposed, thrilling positions, and overcoming not only fatigue of body, but of mind.

When we arrived in the Valley that May of '88, Todd was by far more accomplished at 5.13 climbing. Even though I had established climbs that were 5.12d and had succeeded upon climbs rated 5.13 (but which I could not in good faith believe really were 5.13), Todd was the stronger climber. He had lived on the road, climbing constantly, for years and had given himself the opportunity to continually push his limits. On the other hand, I felt constrained by the usual self-imposed pressures. Every now and then I would throw up my hands and disappear among the rocks for extended and intensive bursts of climbing. But I had never really traveled year-round. Since I had not given myself the opportunity to truly develop my potential, I was sometimes, but not always, playing catch-up to the current standards, rather than actually creating them as Todd had done.

I remember one clear and starry night—Todd and I were sitting in the alcove, below El Cap Spire, halfway up The Salathé. Jotting on the inside covers and the backs of Edgar Rice Burroughs's *Thuvia, Maid of Mars*, we made a list of all the 5.13s that we had successfully climbed. While my list was extremely short at that time, Todd had climbed close to a hundred in the United States and Europe! A remarkable achievement, even now—never mind 1988.

So, his experience was far greater than mine at climbs within the 5.13 grade. Even so, we were an exceptionally well-balanced team. I was extremely solid on 5.12 cracks and had strong face-climbing skills as well. But, more than anything, my contribution was creativity. I was the choreographer of the Free Salathé and Todd was the dancer. Often the composer does not play his composition as beautifully as the musician. One person's skill lies in envisioning, creating, and solving, while the other person's talent lies in perfectly performing the piece. This is not to say that Todd is not creative. On the contrary, he is more creative than almost any climber I have met in America. But at the major impasses on The Salathé, we were pleased that I was able to figure out more quickly than Todd the most efficient and often very clever sequences to the crux

Bridging between the main wall and the hundred-foot-tall El Cap Spire, Paul makes his way toward the summit of this pinnacle which, at 1,700 feet, is the halfway point on the climb.

pitches. Todd, with his much broader base of 5.13, could then more rapidly and perfectly perform the dance that I had discovered . . . and it was a beautiful thing to watch.

I was not unproductive on the performance end, leading one of the 5.13 pitches and my share of the rest. But certainly the pitches that took me many tries to choreograph in pieces would have taken me many more days to lead completely free. Todd's vast level of experience on the hardest pitches shone through and, as a result, he was the stronger climber on three of the four 5.13 pitches. It worked out extremely well that I was faster in sequencing and Todd was faster at putting together the leads.

Due to the wide variety of experiences both of us had given ourselves by traveling as frequently as possible to many different climbing areas, both of us had at our disposal a wide variety of techniques that we had learned in disparate areas. This "library" of moves and techniques proved critical to our success on The Salathé. As much as anything else, we were able to refrain from pronouncing a particular crux section of the climb as "a crack climb," or as "a face climb." The ability to instinctively and simultaneously call into play face climbing, crack climbing, and flare climbing was the key to solving what more traditional crack climbers saw as improbable sections.

In June 1995, an incredibly strong German climber named Alex Huber made the second free ascent of the Salathé Wall. He skipped the first 5.13 pitch in favor of a much easier 5.12a variation which Todd and I had top-roped but rejected, due not only to the unpleasant character of the climbing, but also because we knew the original way was possible. We could not shirk the challenge. Alex made several significant contributions to the evolution of the Free Salathé. Most impressive of these is that he led each pitch. This illustrates the advancement in belief and in endurance that climbers have experienced since 1988.

Except for the 5.13 pitch below, the lion's share of the difficult climbing is yet to come.

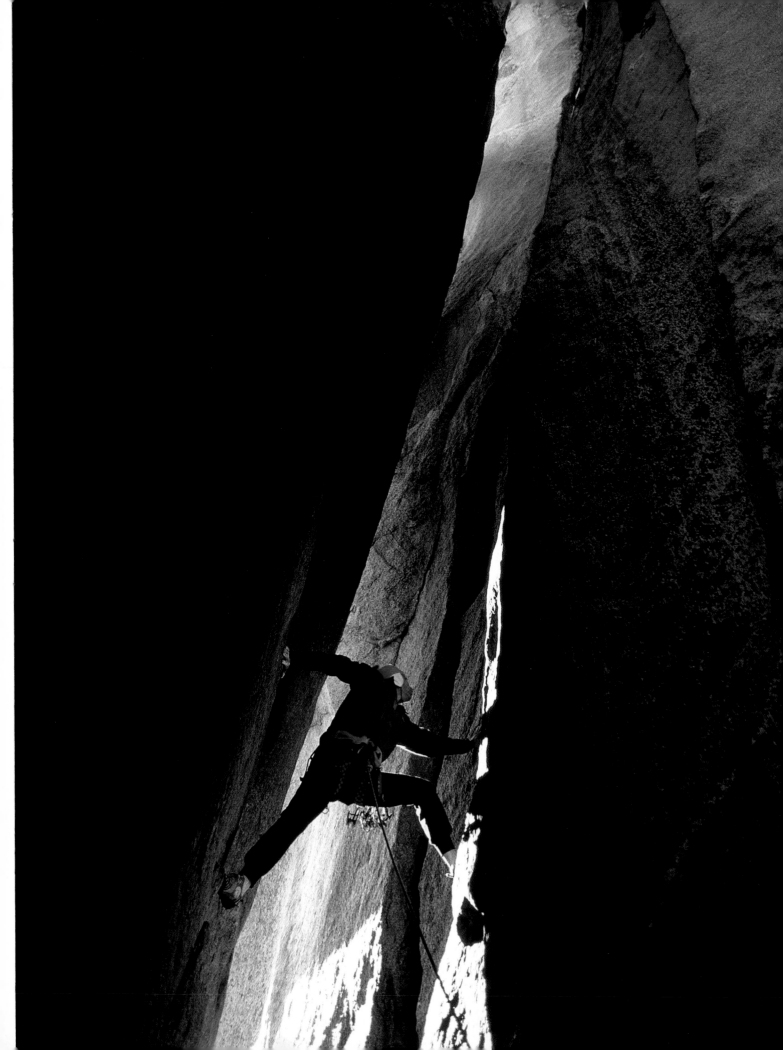

MOUNT HOOKER

VI, 5.12a

The majestic North Face of Mount Hooker stands proudly against the Wyoming sky. While a pretty alpine tarn laps the talus at the wall's base, a pair of Indian Paintbrush, Wyoming's state flower, spices a carpet of wildflowers. The route we would follow on our 1990 First Free Ascent ascent of this 2,000-foot wall follows the approximate line between sun and shadow.

ALONG, LONG TIME AGO—a time of innocence, a time of dreams that we knew would come true because we were strong and young and bold enough to dream them—we followed our dreams onto the sharp feldspar crystals of the Needles and the twisting jams of Devils Tower's unending columns.

While planning our first trip to the real mountains—the Tetons—we came across a darkened photo in Bonney's *Guide to the Wyoming Mountains* . . . a picture of a figure hanging on the side of a sheer wall in a hammock! Even though the photo was poorly reproduced, we could see brave eyes under the visor of a white flat-cap. Someday we would know more about what steeled such confidence into those eyes.

I know it was a long time ago that Todd Skinner and I first discussed Mount Hooker. A long time ago, Todd didn't curse like a drunken sailor when he fell off a hard move, he still considered salami and hard bread to be the perfect meal, and he still carried—and had occasional use for—a small pocket comb.

We bouldered hard in the tunnels that connect the dorms at the University of Wyoming. Late into the nights and early mornings we sat up and hatched plans for projects yet to come.

One night Todd accosted me with a thick, well-thumbed book. The evangelical fire in his eyes bade me step back a pace or two and wonder whether he had suddenly gotten some kind of snakebite religion. He thrust the opened book into my face

and there were the brave eyes, Royal Robbins's, and a description of the north face of Mount Hooker. Pulled from behind this missal of routes and rocks was the epistle *Advanced Rockcraft*, in which Royal Robbins proclaimed Hooker to have a "great face." And it was in our backyard.

"Shouldn't we free climb it next summer?"

"Well, yes," I replied. "We oughta take a look."

Because it was in our backyard, and because nobody had ever heard of Mount Hooker, it could wait until the next year. It was the lone black stallion way up in the back canyons that, from time to time, ran briefly among other dreams and riled 'em up, but that we could never quite get motivated to bring in and brand. We let it be.

Finally, in the autumn of '89, sitting out a snowstorm in our tipi, we made a pact that the next August we would make our bid for Mount Hooker. The year passed and the summer months saw me driving back and forth from the Black Hills to a secret limestone crag in Wyoming. In early August, on my way to rendezvous with Todd and Hooker, I stopped in at Vedauwoo to

A fair bit of planning goes into any venture on a wall several thousand feet high—even more so if the wall is twenty miles deep in the wilderness. There's gear to sort, horse-packers to contract, and logistics to calculate, such as how to find the way in and then back out again. Relaxing around the campfire, plotting the route back out of the mountains are (left to right) *Tim Toula, Amy Whisler* (who had hiked in to deliver congratulatory Pop Tarts), *Todd, and Paul.*

Even during the August daytime it was cold. The summery blue Wyoming sky belies the chill of this shaded north wall. At one point, with the sun shining on all sides and Mount Hooker's tempests blasting, it was so cold that Paul remarked, "Let's come back when it's summer."

do a few routes and learned that Annie Whitehouse, with a group of climbers, had just packed in to free Hooker. And a day later, I heard that Mark Rolofson and party had also gone in with three weeks of provisions to free my Mount Hooker. I was crushed, speechless, and depressed.

I met Todd and Tim Toula with a look on my face that must have been deathly: like Casey Tibbs after Freckles Brown rode Tornado — or my dad as he walked my sister down the wedding aisle. We were frantic. We called Michael Kennedy and asked

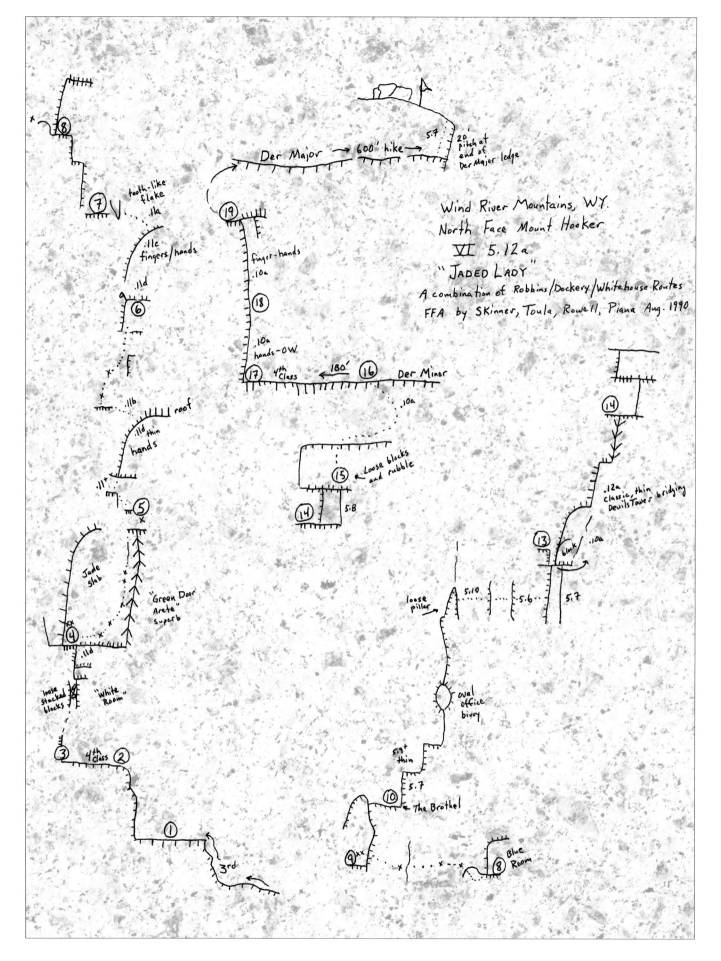

Der Major → 600' hike →

5.7

20' pitch at end of Der Major ledge

Wind River Mountains, W.Y.
North Face Mount Hooker
VI 5.12a
"JADED LADY"
A combination of Robbins/Dockery/Whitehouse Routes
FFA by Skinner, Toula, Rowell, Piana Aug. 1990

tooth-like flake
.11a

.11c fingers/hands

.11d

finger-hands
.10a

.10a
hands-OW

4th Class   ←180'→   Der Minor

.10a

Loose blocks and rubble

roof

.11b

.11d thin hands

.11+

Jade Slab

"Green Door Arete" superb

.11d

loose stacked blocks

"White Room"

5.8

.12a classic, thin DevilsTower bridging

block   .10a

loose pillar   5.10 .... 5.6   5.7

oval office bivvy

4th Class

3rd

5.9+ thin

5.7

The Brothel

Blue Room

There were few ledges of any size on this climb. Paul (in yellow) and Tim are waiting on one of the largest in the first 1,500 feet, a ledge four rope-lengths up the big wall.

As the topo map of the free route shows, the character of the climbing is very different from that of Yosemite's walls. Instead of following long crack systems, a free climber on Mt. Hooker must negotiate clever traverses in order to link fissures that are often less than 100-feet in length.

whether he had any "basecamp" scoop on two parties going in to climb our wall, and if he did hear any news, could he please let us know immediately. No word came, so we continued organizing our bags and trying to wrangle a better price out of the horsepackers. Galen Rowell had airline reservations to Wyoming to do the climb with us—should we tell him the trip might be futile? We weren't interested in any second ascent.

We were hanging around our secret crag two days before we were due to hike in, when who should walk up but Annie

I remember how cold it was, always cold—the slow, unrelenting cold that stiffens the backs of your hands inside your gloves and spreads quickly until you are thick and the color of x-rays deep inside. Constantly wearing every stitch of clothing we possessed, we were cold all day and cold, cold at night. I remember the sunlight teasing an edge one hundred feet to the right or floating a glimmer six feet out into the void. And, leaning way out, an ungloved hand would court the slightest touch of gold.

I remember Todd climbing all but two pitches in his Five Tennies and leading one pitch—an eighty-foot, 12a traverse protected with only three pieces of pro—in a wind so brutal that, while belaying, I was plastered against the wall like a wet flag to a building. I marveled at how Todd simultaneously finessed across poor change for a dime while winning a shoving match with an arctic hurricane.

The memories of the bivvy sites stand out, because there were none. Just one hammock would have been worth a million bucks, a porta-ledge a million five. The first night on the wall, Galen crammed into the back of a bottomless, cavelike hole called the "Oval Office." To sleep inside this awful orifice, he wedged himself like a cube in a champagne tulip—he couldn't fall out, but neither could he be comfortable.

While I'm fairly sure that Galen slept poorly, I am absolutely certain that sometime during this life or a past existence, Tim Toula committed an act so nefarious, so eternally heinous, that he was made to endure, as his penance, this first night on Mount Hooker. While Todd and I had to rappel 150 feet and 200 feet, respectively, to suffer like beach balls balanced on World Trade Center windowsills, Tim paid for his sins—and all mankind's since Adam—confined to a "ledge" the size of a paperback book. This feature sloped gently into the void and accommodated about half of one-half of Tim's backside. To keep from falling off, he rigged a sling for his feet off to one side and then, unable to get into his sleeping bag and remain on his perch, he battled gravity, extreme discomfort, cold, and wind through the terrible night. Rapping past

The Green Door is the name of a memorable pitch formed from a deep green type of rock that looks like jade. The climbing on the route follows the jagged edge on the right. In this view Todd, having led the pitch, is hauling up a pack of gear while Paul and Tim await their turn to climb the pitch.

Todd is beginning the smooth jade-colored slab called the Green Door.
The surface of the rock was as slippery as a polished jade carving.

Only where bits of rock had flaked away were there small rough edges which made possible a dance from one to the other, higher and higher.

The 5.12a crux of the route and the most classic pitch on the climb is pitch 14. Tim was lucky enough to win the draw for the lead and skilled enough to finesse his way up. The difficulties of this classic, open book consisted of very steep rock, tiny footholds, and thin fingerlocks. As a bonus, if you are as strong as Tim and can hang around to place it—good protection slotted nicely in this classic and beautiful open book.

Near the top of the Green Door, Paul is moving up the wall by stealthy foot smears on subtle depressions and by pulling on a crack and the edge of the Green Door, using hands and arms like ice tongs.

"Slack on the black rope! . . ." One of the funny yet annoying blunders we made was taking along one blue rope and three black ropes. A couple of times, monumental tangles resulted from losing track of several coils to the wind. The Gordian knot that Paul is unbraiding is Mount Hooker's version of Rubik's Cube.

edge of Hooker's eastern visage—a little-known 1,000-foot iron curtain—we lollygagged down steep slopes to basecamp. There we were met by Amy Whisler, who had walked in twenty-one miles to surprise us with strawberry Pop Tarts. Our catered celebration was Pop Tarts chased down by two giant cans of Toula-supplied Fosters Lager.

(right) Galen's camera flash lit the darkness and shows Todd wedged, back and knee, in the "oval office." Todd's job as chef was to balance the tortillas on his knees and portion out the evening's meal. Tim, Galen, and Paul hung from ropes outside the teardrop-shaped hole in the rock while Todd deftly whittled cheese in the darkness, and, one at a time, passed out his special Mount Hooker Tuna burritos!

We had survived the cold, the wind, and huge, loose blocks to come away with a grand prize: the first free ascent of America's finest alpine wall. Tomorrow we would begin the long march out, bearing 400 pounds of gear. In the meantime, the beer had gone to our heads and the campfire was warm. Life was exactly the way it should be and, smug with success, we started laying plans to rope in a few more dreams and shake them by the scruff of the neck until they came true.

MOUNT HOOKER POSTSCRIPT

Todd belays as Tim leads, high on the steep side of Mount Hooker. Twenty miles beyond the climbers, in the plains to the east of these Wind River Mountains, is the town of Lander, Wyoming, where Todd and Paul live. Lander nestles too close to the foothills to see many of the high peaks, but twenty-five miles farther east, nearer Riverton, Wyoming, the black shield that is the North Face of Mount Hooker can easily be seen.

MOUNT HOOKER IS LESS than twenty air miles from my home in Lander, Wyoming. From our small-town airport, the little planes that buzz off the runways can spy its walls just minutes after takeoff. It is a remarkable facet of the Wind River Mountains, and were it in any other state, it would undoubtedly be traced by far more routes than the five or so that exist.

For Todd and me, this climb was very satisfying, as it was the second listed on our Four Great Walls to be free climbed. It was enjoyable to be climbing with our friends Tim Toula and Galen Rowell. Our climb was plagued by the wind and

After leading across this traverse, Todd said he felt that the hardest part of this 5.12a pitch was not so much the technical difficulty as it was enduring the bitter chill of the wind while fighting to stay balanced on small edges and friction holds. This shot shows him "plastered against the wall like a wet flag to a building."

In this view down the crux pitch, Todd has laybacked through the initial roof and is beginning the fingertip jamming and toetip balancing to follow Tim's lead. At this point, the climbers have reached the 1,400-foot level on the 2,000-foot wall.

cold rather than cruxes. Since our free climb of Mount Hooker and the appearance of my story (originally titled "This Hooker's History") in *Rock & Ice* magazine, many climbers have called asking about my recommendations for horsepackers or for the usual what-should-I-take sorts of queries. All of them have assumed that I had exaggerated about how cold it could be on that north-facing wall. All of them who have climbed the wall have come back sorry they hadn't believed my descriptions of

"the slow, unrelenting cold that stiffens the backs of your hands inside your gloves and spreads quickly until you are thick and the color of X-rays deep inside."

We were very lucky to have gotten away with free climbing Mount Hooker, as we were too late in the season, and had unbelievably good weather compared to what was possible. We were also lucky to have had a topo given to us by Annie White-house, Stuart Ritchie, and Mark Rolofson. They had gone to Mount Hooker to attempt a free ascent of the Robbins Route. They came out a few days before we were scheduled to go in. Their route, which they named The Jaded Lady (after a re-markable hundred-foot-high jade-colored slab which forms one of the pitches), was obvious up to a point. At this point, the rock directly above was probably climbable, but at a high standard. There, the team made a clever, eighty-foot traverse to the left into a crack system which soon joined the Robbins Route; a reasonable free passage to the summit. In these five or six pitches of new climbing, the team fixed fifteen bolts, mostly for protection. Everything was going well for them until pitch 14.

It's early in the morning. The sun is hitting the talus and the tarn below, but as usual, its warmth is far from our perch on the wall. We're halfway up, and it's time to climb, but not until we share a swallow of water and some chocolate-covered espresso beans.

From the time we stepped off the talus until we unroped on the sunny summit, we were cold. Always teased by the sun, which never quite warmed the rock, Paul leans out from his belay anchors, straining for a touch of the sun.

Rain hit the party and Mark Rolofson, who was leading, found the rock too wet to free climb. They report that they were low on water and out of food on their third day and, rather than wait to try to climb the dihedral in dry conditions, decided to aid the pitch and escape upward.

On our climb we marveled at the climbability of the rock, at the horribly loose sections of certain flake systems, at the cold, and how surprised we were that our three predecessors had given up so easily. Even though the dihedral on pitch 14 was wet, there were a couple of easier and quick-to-dry alternatives. I'm certain that they have since been sorry that they did not persevere and suffer just a litle bit longer. In my *Rock & Ice* article, I did not go into great detail about how many bolts they had placed, or that they had given us a topo of their route. I did write, however, that pitch 14 was the only section of the wall that they had failed to free climb, and that the dihedral was the line that made their free attempt into an aid climb. I do know that Annie and Mark were upset with me, as evidenced by the heated letters they wrote to the climbing media in which they claimed that I had misconstrued facts and omitted information that would have given them more credit. With the 20/20 vision of hindsight, and given the vituperative letters they wrote, it seems clear that I should have written a little more about their climb and should have given them more recognition for crafting the variation that made our free climb of the wall easier.

Their Jaded Lady variation was a good effort that allowed a free route at a reasonable grade to be established on Mount Hooker. I did not wish to imply that their route was an experiential failure, or that they were not clever in route finding, or that they were poor climbers, or anything else against them. I did, however, wish to convey that we did the first free ascent. If we had failed to free climb fifty feet (or even one move) of the route on Mount Hooker, we would have considered our climb a failure. On the other hand, with their ascent of a fine and clever variation and as a great adventure among friends, their climb up the wall of Mount Hooker was (for them, I hope) a huge success.

Paul's favorite shot of Mount Hooker. To take this photo, Galen had to get up pretty darned early on a cold morning, hike more than a mile from camp, and wait for the brief moment when the first sun rays burned the great wall red.

Todd and Paul were very, very happy to have free climbed what they consider the finest wilderness big wall in "the lower 48," and to have shared the experience with two great friends.

MOUNT HOOKER OCCUPIES a cold spot on the planet, but it holds a warm spot in our hearts. It is the greatest big wall in our home state of Wyoming. It is one of the premier big walls in North America. It is the site of America's first grade VI rock climb on a remote big wall, and, of course, the site of the first free ascent of a grade VI wilderness rock climb in America. Because Mount Hooker is in our backyard and because it was the second success on our list of the four greatest big walls in America, it will always remain special to us.

Whenever I think of Mount Hooker, I do not choose to remember it as the cold and harsh environment of our climb, but as the huge monolith of Galen's photo—smoldering like a coal in the early morning light. I choose to remember the warmth of the summit sunlight and the satisfaction of success on that wildflower-strewn mountaintop. I choose to remember the mischievous glint in Tim's eyes as he pulled the Fosters out of his pack and the crackling taste of those celebratory beers we shared at our campfire the night after our climb.

I choose to put aside the memories of bitter cold, of leaden doubt, of the little fears of being so far off the ground. I choose to remember only the parts that make me feel good about these climbs: the friendship, the athleticism, the invigorating views, and the sweet reward of success hard earned.

The obligatory summit photo. As soon as we stepped into the sun on this flower-strewn mountaintop, we were warm once again.

THE GREAT CANADIAN KNIFE

VI, 5.13b

In an early morning view of Mount Proboscis, the dramatic line of "The Great Canadian Knife" can be seen cutting directly up the center of the wall.

THERE ARE DREAMS THAT become goals and, for most people, these goals remain mere dreams. Dreams remain safe and unchanging, with no horrors like failure to get in the way. Throughout the 1960s, the climber with the greatest desire to realize his dreams of climbing the greatest lines on the greatest rock walls was Royal Robbins.

Royal and his peers had to be artistic enough to dream big, inventive enough to figure out new techniques to use on big walls, and bold enough to fight their way up them. They had to be sufficiently bulletproof, or at least not bleed in public.

"Where Royal Robbins has driven his pitons, we will endeavor to fingerlock!" This is our credo and our game plan. From our success on The Salathé and later on Mount Hooker, we became convinced that every wall worth freeing was first ascended by Royal and friends.

(right) The rock in the Cirque of the Unclimbables was festooned with edges, crystals, and knobs, as well as being cut by cracks. This meant we were able to free climb what, at first glance, looked impossibly smooth. The potential was so ripe for high-standard climbs that Todd joked about renaming the place "Cirque of the FreeClimbables."

Of the first ascent of the South East Face of Proboscis, in his book *Beyond the Vertical*, Layton Kor writes:

In 1963 Yvon Chouinard published his now classic article in the *American Alpine Club Journal* which concluded, "The future of Yosemite climbing lies not in Yosemite, but in using the new techniques in the great granite ranges of the world." That same year the American Alpine Club began a program of "vigorous encouragement of modern technical climbing in North America." Jim McCarthy was asked by the AAC "to pick an objective that you feel will contribute something to the development of

American climbing, gather the strongest group of technical climbers available to do the job, and the AAC will back the venture." McCarthy selected the South East Face of Mount Proboscis in the Cirque of the Unclimbables in the Logan Mountains of the North West Territories of Canada—an enormous face in a remote location. The team comprised McCarthy, Royal Robbins, Dick McCracken, and myself, and... was to result in the first Yosemite style Grade VI on such a remote mountain face.

Jim McCarthy was so excited telling us about Proboscis that I thought he might burst. He was waving his arms and rocking back and forth, hysterical as a snakebite evangelist. His eyes were starting to bug out as he remembered the ecstasy of the first ascent. He rocked up, rising onto his toes, and mimed the angle of the wall with his hands. "The face is sooo steep..." He rolled back on his heels. "It's overhanging... it snowed on us, and it rained on us and none of us got wet." In his excitement, Mac was leaning so far, I didn't see what was holding him up. "It's so friggin' big, man . . ." His euphoric gaze was snapping back and forth from Todd, to Galen, to me. "If you think you want to make a mark, you better go up there and try that one."

We thought it might be nice to drive all the way, and piled a huge amount of equipment and rations into Galen's Suburban. All the way up Galen regaled us with stories of his first trips into these regions, tales of climbs and great climbers. We loved the stories and the frequent stops to take photos of mountains and the unending clear-cuts of British Columbia. From Calgary to Watson Lake is 1,700 miles of rainy-day driving through verdant forests and beautiful mountains. We would toss a sleeping bag beside the car at night and then drive into the next frontier town for roadhouse coffee.

Somewhere almost 300 kilometers north of the town of Watson Lake we turned off the road at a previously arranged mileage marker. Warren La Fave thundered out of the sky and splashed down for a landing on Finlayson Lake. We loaded his immaculate de Havilland Beaver float plane and skimmed up

The great Italian alpinist Emilio Comici once said "I wish someday to make a route and from the summit drop a drop of water; this is where my route will have gone." Perhaps anticipating this Comici ideal, Mother Nature honed the 1,500 foot blade of The Great Canadian Knife.

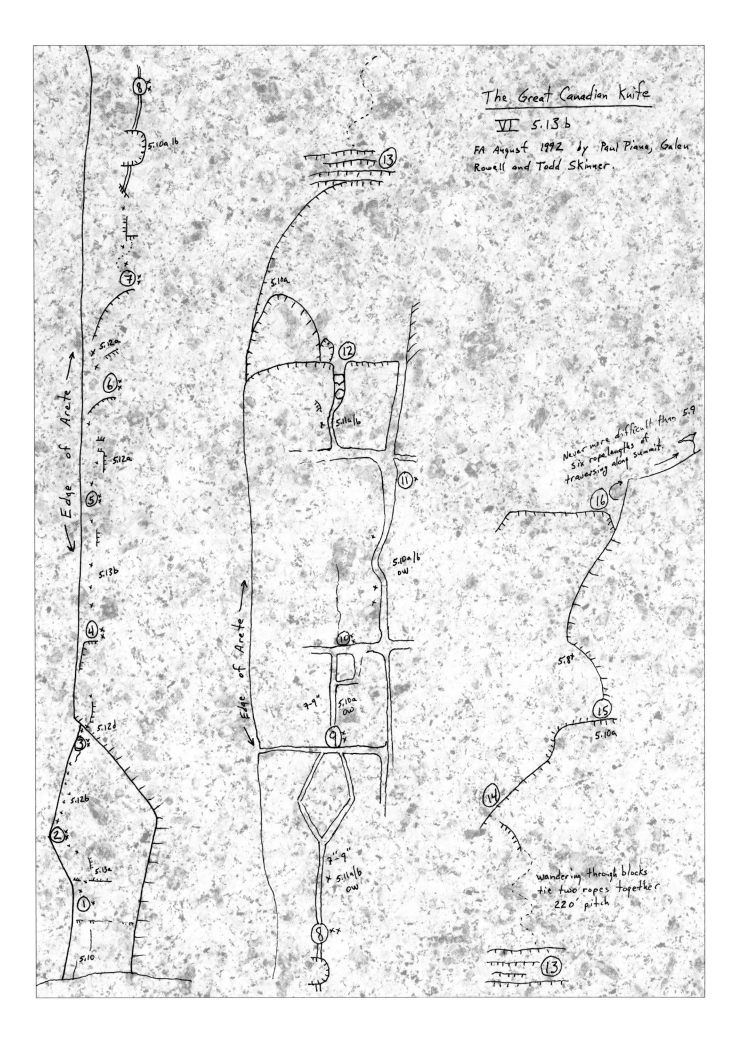

The Great Canadian Knife

VI 5.13b

FA August 1992 by Paul Piana, Galen
Rowell and Todd Skinner.

Never more difficult than 5.9
Six ropelengths of
traversing along summit.

Wandering through blocks
tie two ropes together
220' pitch

At the 1,200-foot level, we moved into the crack systems just to the right of the Knife's edge and followed them to their end on a large shelf, which is where, due to foreshortening, the summit appears to be.

LTHOUGH IT WAS A PARTY from Barcelona, Spain, we were wrong about who the climbers were. A Spaniard calling himself Husa, along with Joachin Olmo and Friederike Wellmer, turned out to be darned nice camping companions and became super friends. Our new neighbors had visited the Cirque of the Unclimbables the previous season and, upon flying out, had been able to look over at a mountain they had never even heard of. In a Catalonian exclamation, they said, "Woooow! What's that?! Next year we're gonna do whatever that is!" They returned and had selected a line right up the middle which became "Costa Brava" (VI 5.10+ A3). Their route was a variant of the South East Face Route pioneered by Robbins, Kor, McCarthy, and McCracken in 1963. They chose to climb a "Stove-leg-Crack-like" feature, just to the left of the faint knifeblade line that had been favored by the 1963 team.

When we spied them, they were coming down for the day. We discussed the fact that we had come to free the wall via the line they were on and they said, "No problem! We are having fun, and we are sure you won't be in the way." While Galen visited with our new friends, Todd and I hiked up the talus with some gear. We were intent upon getting the use out of every available daylight hour. Both of us looked at the Robbins line for a while, and then walked left a couple hundred yards to the base of a feature I had first seen on page 53 of Kor's *Beyond the Vertical*. In Wyoming we had gazed at photos and wondered about the feature, which I began calling "The Great Canadian Knife." It was the most architecturally perfect feature we had ever seen on a mountain . . . a clean, overhanging arete; as aesthetic as a corner of the Chrysler Building, but much taller. We realized that we would rather fail attempting to free climb this immense knife blade than succeed on the

Looking up at Paul ascending fixed lines on the 2,000-foot-high South East Face of Mount Proboscis. Route-finding on the Great Canadian Knife is easy; the 1,500-foot-long arete delineates the first three-fourths of the climb.

think, drilled a bat-hook and had me lower him, so that he could pendulum farther left to another flake which was rotten but climbable. From its top, a few more hook moves led to the belay. I was freaking out, just jugging that pitch. If anything had popped prior to the belay, Todd would still be falling.

At the end of the climbing day, which, at the earliest, was usually about 11:00 P.M., we would rap fixed lines in the last, midnight light to visit our Catalonian friends. One day, Friederike asked me, "Were you crying? We were watching you with binoculars and saw you fall and heard you crying." I explained to her that I was hooking through the only roof of the climb. I had hooked out the roof to a place from which I could reach over and grab the bottom of a flake system. From the tops of my stirrups, I reached up and jammed in a 2 1/2 Friend. Relieved, I clipped in my stirrups and climbed high onto them using the flake as a lieback. Unfortunately, the insides of these flakes were often rotten. With an attention-getting *grro-ott* sound, the Friend sheared. I heard my heart pounding in my head and felt some super-electric, shrieking wail course down my spine and I stopped falling and began arcing back and forth, level with Todd. I was carefully explaining to Freidereke that she may have heard the wind slicing across the sharp summit of Proboscis, but that fellas from Wyoming never, ever cry. But I don't think she properly translated what I said, because she replied, "No, you were crying when you fell . . . it was a very good fall." But all I really remember was the rushing vacuum, the electric pressure and then the creaking from a rocking, cobra-shaped hook.

Fingers crimping on sugar cube-sized holds, Paul is embroiled in the 5.12 difficulties of the bulging fourth pitch.

DURING THE FIRST DAYS, as Todd and I were preparing the route, we would hear a faint *whoop* and look around, squinting hard, to spy a tiny Galen silhouette atop a summit, or calling from the ridge off to our left. On many mornings, Galen was up and away before us and wouldn't be seen until well after dark. As to where he had been, he would offhandedly reply, "Well, I haven't been here in twenty-three years, so I thought I'd hike over to the Lotus

In this photo, Paul is seen on the final moves of the third pitch. The climbing on this 5.12b lead was the first of several that climbed directly on the blade of the arete. At times hands and feet were used to pinch together on the very edge, climbing like a South Seas native might shimmy up a palm tree.

Flower Tower. I think I'll go back again tomorrow." Never mind the fact that Lotus Flower Tower is in the third valley over and to reach it from our camp requires plenty of serious alpine climbing. From experience, we knew that Galen was a dynamo, but his unrelenting drive and enthusiasm astounded our Catalonian friends.

As soon as we had fixed five rope-lengths up the wall, we began to work and equip pitches. Our concerns in freeing these big walls have evolved over the years. What we consider

The desperate climbing on the Great Canadian Knife began with the second pitch. Todd is seen on the sharp end of the rope, having dispensed with the 5.13a crux, as well as the 5.12 section, and is intently pulling through the remaining 5.11 face moves to reach the belay.

This photo is Paul's favorite from the climb, as to him it best conveys what it felt like to climb on that wild and airy razor's edge.

Galen's photo provides a remarkable view down the very edge of the Great Canadian Knife, as Todd is seen climbing the rope length that turned out to be the 5.13b crux of the entire route.

In this second view of the fourth pitch, Paul has successfully climbed through the lead's desperate crux and is preparing to launch up the overhanging 5.12a power pulls between flakes.

Even though it rained or snowed almost every day we climbed on this route, the overhanging nature of the wall sheltered us from everything except a little windblown moisture.

to be good style is simply the end product. If at any point we can no longer free climb, we abandon the climb, since aiding to the top is meaningless. We choose only the most beautiful climbs and ascend them in such a way that future ascents need never utilize scarring techniques such as pitons or bashies. For Todd and me, aid climbs are anachronisms. We believe the future of the sport lies in free climbing, and that hammered protection must be used only to protect free climbs. It must be judiciously placed to be as strong and long-lived as technology allows. One stainless steel 3/8" bolt is worth more than ten rusty pitons, and environmental change stops occurring after the first ascent. With this in mind, we carefully considered each placement with regard to location, utility, and aesthetics.

We were lucky with the weather. Even though it rained or snowed a little every day, we remained dry due to the steepness of the wall. For two days, however, we were tent-bound and feared that we would wash away. Our amigos gifted us with 200 meters of static rope, which meant we could fix much higher. We were very happy to have this luxury of living on the ground. We employed it immediately and began working our way up the wall, first aiding each pitch, and then freeing it. We were climbing as continuously as we would have been with wall bivvys, but were enjoying it a whole lot more.

Now that we were getting to free climb, we found that we were having a really good time. The audacious feature we were slowly free climbing was providing us with surprisingly varied pitches. The second pitch was an Eldorado-esque wonder. It began with an overhanging bulge stacked with all sorts of trick moves: hard-to-hold crimpers, hand pops to side pulls, followed by long surges into gymnastic dismount positions held by thumb hooks in the bottoms of flakes. This first of two 5.13 pitches on the route was Todd's initial free face-off on the

Another view of Todd climbing above the dizzy drop on this incredible route.

Good morning! A bird's-eye view from Galen's porta-ledge down to the ledge shared by Paul and Todd. This hanging camp is halfway up the wall — a thousand feet above the snow at the base.

What made the fifth pitch so desperate was the unrelentingly tenuous nature of the climbing. Rather than alternating hard parts and less difficult stretches, the pitch kept trying to toss the climber into space for its entire length. The very edge of the Knife was Todd's left handhold throughout most of the pitch, while his right hand had to utilize much smaller pickings.

Great Canadian Knife. He danced, parried, and came away without a scratch. The sword fighter's smirk was long on his face.

The fourth pitch roof was mine. After Todd had seen me lob-off the thing and end up swinging from the hook that caught my fall, he was anxious that I get the sharp end. The beginning was sharp and dynamic, as I was too short to reach between lousy holds. At the end of the 5.12d section, I became aware of Galen dangling out in space and muttering that he had run out of film. I kept climbing. I was astounded a few weeks later, when we viewed the slides at Galen's studio in Berkeley. He had changed film with the speed of light; there was no break in the almost motor-drive sequence documenting that pitch.

Looking down what was to be the crux of the route, Galen photographed the most abstract lead of the climb. As Todd began, his hand clasped the blade of the arete, which at that point was only a degree or two steeper than vertical. The rock was honed as smooth as granite can get without being polished. The dizzy drop was accentuated by the sudden edge. Todd's feet had to smear so powerfully, the slight depressions

he stood on were deepened by the force of his climbing shoes. I had worked this 5.13b pitch, so I knew that Todd might deal successfully with the crux, but take a beating from the remaining 5.12+. Flawless movement using slick knobs like they were buckets saw him through all of the horror sections. Todd had only one more 5.12a step onto the arete and an easy flake. I knew that Todd had prematurely dropped his guard; he was tensing up, hesitating. By now it was late in the day and we had time for only this try. With the fickle weather, we needed every effort to be efficient. And due to the late hour and the sun being off the rock, a little ooze had seeped out of a flake and

This incredible photo, taken while Todd and Paul slept, is the result of Galen's untiring quest to record his impressions of beautiful places. Galen must be a new species of human—one that never rests and requires less sleep than any other mammal.

Down valley and away to the south of Mount Proboscis, a glaciated wonderland of alps provided a scene so beautiful it almost made Todd and Paul want to resume snow and ice climbing.

dripped onto the key foothold. Pessimism shook me. I was resigned to trying tomorrow, but Todd spat an invective so hot it temporarily dried the foothold and strained so hard between iron-cross thumb hooks that I could see muscles bunch through his pile shirt. Todd had climbed gracefully up to this point, but now was as jittery as a telegraph key. In an impressive demonstration of thrashing that began with a sort of trap-door yelp and a technique that could be likened to a haul bag following a pendulum, he lunged across . . . and held on! Surprised and shaking, Todd lurched to the belay just as the sun's glow faded into the short, far north night.

The sun's dip into cobalt began to lighten almost as soon as evening began. Even so, for a few intimidating hours, Proboscis was cast in a dead-skin, platinum pallor and stood cold and aloof. During those silent hours I was afraid whenever I looked up at the wall. During those hours I tried to sleep and to recover. Just as I could doze, morning would slowly be born. Then Galen would disappear with his camera gear to document the blue- and rose-colored hour. In the sunlight I was brave again.

WE KNEW THAT ATOP PITCH seven there was a monstrous flake. This massive stone door was eight feet high, four feet wide, and fifteen inches thick. It had a TV-sized rock behind, and the big menace leaned drunkenly into the void. The night before, we had warned everyone on the ground that we were going to push off a big, big rock. Since the Great Canadian Knife is such a laser-straight line, we hauled up the fixed lines to the belay. We screamed "RAW-AACK!!!" in every language we knew. We got ready to push like hell, as we didn't want the big palooka to rock back and rub us out. "Okay, on 'three,' " we agreed. We reached out, put our hands on it, chanted, "One . . . Two . . ." and with an insignificant little grinding sound, we watched it swan-dive into the great Canadian void. At the instant the rock fell, time slowed and the world was suddenly so quiet that I knew there would never again be sound. No wind. No hollow hush of breathing. No nothing. For five eternally silent minutes, we watched it fall and fall and fall . . . turning and gliding as if it were a giant leaf. A hundred feet off the talus, it slowly banked and kamikazied into the wall, spewing slow motion shrapnel far across the talus. We waited for the lack of sound to quickly fill in, for the crash to catch up, flooding our great, quiet, and scared reality.

Our team had reached a place on the wall where it was necessary to make a route-finding decision. The choice was to continue climbing the very blade of the arete or to veer up and right, into a crack system that ended on the same ledge. All of us wished to continue up the strong line, but our supply of bolts was almost spent. We reluctantly forsook the arete and began climbing the cracks.

Our first bivvy on the wall was here. We slung porta-ledges 1,200 feet up and dreamed our wildest dreams. The visions were steel blue, glinting colors, and forever gray voids. Real-life winds rose up and pummeled the porta-ledges, thrumming the flies like runaway jib sails. The wind punched us from below, then dropped us back down. The night seemed colder, meaner, and longer than usual.

W HEN MORNING CAME, I began leading and whooping that if the rest of the crack system was this grand, we were in for a fun-fest. Todd's lead was next, and the crack seemed to widen higher up. His hand-crack slowly became off-hands, then fist jamming and then bigger. His disappointment turned to swearing as he thrashed higher, learning that he lacked the proper sized protection for these seven- to nine-inch cracks. Fortunately, Galen owned a seven-inch Big-Dude, which Todd managed to place about sixty feet up the lead. He hung from the piece, pulled the drill,

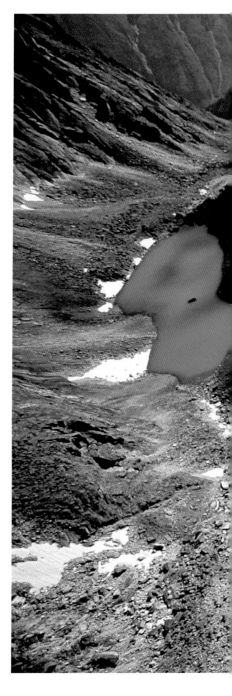

Above our hanging camp, we soon entered a crack system several hundred feet long, which ended on the same ledge where our amazing arete terminated. Paul's lead began with a couple of hard face-climbing moves, but was mostly fun 5.10 hand-jamming up to a layback flake and a belay.

sunk some solid protection, and climbed on. After a ninety-foot runout the crack narrowed again, enabling Todd to repeat the procedure, establishing a belay. He rappelled off and joined us at our belay. While Todd rested, Galen took the opportunity to jug to the belay Todd had just established. Galen then photographed Todd's free-lead of the first of several off-width pitches.

Rising above one belay was a fissure just wide enough that you hoped you could squeeze inside, but no matter how hard you struggled, it wouldn't let you in. Even worse, the crack exhibited an overhanging S-curve section. Galen commented that it looked easier than off-widths he had led twenty-five years

The crack system that began for Paul as fun, hand-sized jams soon got wider and wider for Todd, who had to struggle up a seven- to nine-inch off-width-sized crack which for the most part was unprotected.

earlier. The wind was howling and Galen was bitching about his jackets restricting him. As he led into the S-curve overhang, his hat rubbed against the rock above and turned over his face, obscuring his vision. I would have laughed, but he was easily twenty feet above his last pro, and began a frantic, twitching kick. I got ready to photograph a spectacular fall sequence, but Galen composed his breathing, let a hand loose to readjust his hat and calmly climbed to the pitch's end. All Galen was concerned about was whether or not I had gotten any pictures. I told him, "Not ones I thought I was going to get!" Galen replied, "It wasn't very hard—only 5.10b," with the conviction of a man holding only aces.

I decided to pitch a coiled 9mm rope that I didn't want to lug to the top. I took it to the edge, held it out, and let go. The rope fell, never touching the wall, until it splattered into the snow field, twelve feet out from the starting moves. The hour was late, and we still had five hundred feet to go to the top of the wall. A lot of it was pretty easy. We kept racing upward into the night. At the end of pitch 16, Todd yelled down that he had found an "interesting" bivouac. We had reached the crest of the Proboscis axe blade. Within inches, the mountain changed directions from up to down, and dropped off to the north.

We carefully draped ourselves like saddle blankets over the summit ridge. As usual, Galen was firing off photos, his flash strobing away the blackness. I don't remember ever going to sleep, as I was always cold. There was a space in time when I no longer heard the whir of a Nikon motor drive, and yet, long before I awakened, I heard it; *clickzzz, clickzzz* . . . I peeked from inside my cinched-shut sleeping bag and could see frost riming the opening to the bivvy sack . . . *clickzzz, clickzzz* . . . I dared a one-eyed look at the source of the constant *clickzzz* sound and there was Galen, his hands as blue and as stiff as a frozen rope, miserably ecstatic to be photographing the play of mountain light and the jet abstraction of shadows.

*The ridge crest of the summit provided easy climbing —
mostly scrambling with occasional short steps down and back
up the notches in the top of this gigantic granite wall.*

A S MORNING LIGHT WAS SHOWING us our spectacularly ridiculous bivvy spot, we wrestled ourselves out of cramped positions and began our climb across the top of the wall. For seven rope lengths we traversed along a summit so sharp that we used it as a handrail. Occasional gaps provided minor difficulties and required climbing down and back up the other side. We rambled along in our Five Tennies, laughing and examining pitons from the previous two ascents of the Buckingham West Ridge Route. Eventually we reached a spot where the handrail widened to sidewalk width and remained that wide until it suddenly fell into the cirques containing Bustle and Lotus Flower Towers. Midway along this walkway was a cairn and in it, a small film canister containing the signatures of many of Todd's and my greatest heroes: Bill Buckingham, Tom and Doreen Frost, Sandy Bill, and, of course, the first ascensionists of the South East Face, Jim McCarthy, Layton Kor, Richard McCracken, and Royal Robbins. It was one of my dreams come true — to climb in this majestic range. It was another to make the first free ascent of Proboscis. But the wildest of them all had come true: that I would be fortunate enough to make the first ascent of such a magnificent line as the Great Canadian Knife. It was a bonus to have the route turn out to be the best climb of my life!

The three of us were glowing in the long day's sun. We were ecstatic. Todd and I were pleased beyond words to be huddled around the cairn with our legendary partner, a contemporary of the heroes whose names were in the summit register. Galen fumbled around in his jacket pocket and tore off a piece of a Climbing magazine envelope that he found there. We watched as one of this area's pioneers wrote a brief description of the Great Canadian Knife, VI, 5.13b. We were honored to add our names alongside his and the climbers who have so profoundly inspired us. I will never forget the great pleasure of

At the far east end of Mount Proboscis's summit, where it drops dramatically into the next cirque, is a hundred-foot-long section that is as wide as a sidewalk. Here on this rare perch we found a film canister set in a small cairn which contained the signatures of some of our greatest heroes. We imagined their long-ago moments of jubilation when, like now, the mountains rang with the joy of backslapping and laughter.

This telephoto, taken from across the valley, shows Paul (above) belaying Todd as he sequences the fifth and most difficult pitch on the climb.

standing atop this most beautiful climb, of slapping each other on the back and wondering aloud: "Which Robbins Wall shall we free next?"

GREAT CANADIAN KNIFE POSTSCRIPT

THE GREAT CANADIAN KNIFE is the highest quality wall route I have ever done, seen, or envisioned. Everything about the climb was perfect, from the bold line it cut—up one of the big walls of legend to the surreal region in which it is located, to the quality of the climbing we encountered en route.

There are many incredible and wild places I have been fortunate to visit. Many of them, while beautiful and fascinating, never quite lived up to the photographs that lured me to them to begin with. The Cirque of the Unclimbables however, was everything I had hoped it would be. All of it was just the same as I had seen it in Galen's book *Mountain Light*. The gargoyle boulders in emerald green meadows below the Lotus Flower

THE DIRECT
NORTH WEST FACE
OF HALF DOME

VI, 5.13d

Half Dome, a fantastic and sublime mountain which is one of the symbols of Yosemite National Park. This 2,700-foot North West Face of Half Dome has several times been the scene of breakthroughs in the attitudes and techniques of climbing. The entire course of the Direct North West Face Route can be followed by dropping a plumb line down the face from the left edge of The Visor, which is the overhang at the very summit.

MAYBE IT WAS TAKEN FROM an old issue of *Summit*, or from the pages of the classic Chouinard Equipment Company's catalog advocating a switch from pitons to nuts. "It" was a black-and-white photograph of Royal Robbins snapped in 1963, during the first ascent of the Direct North West Face of Half Dome. In that photo, Royal was camouflaged by a down jacket, white, flat cap, and beard, and bandoliered by slings and pitons and etriers. Royal was standing on a four-inch-wide ledge. A strand of rope arced away, leading his expression to the camera, and his face wore a calm that very few others could have exhibited if it were their heels hanging over thousands of feet of thin Yosemite air.

That picture was carefully cut from the page and used as a sort of name card on my college dormitory room. Of course, everyone in the dorm assumed that the photo was of me, on what they believed were my harrowing ascents. After all, I had a climbing rope, a down jacket, and, if the light was right, a real beard. Unless someone asked, I never pointed out that the photo was not of me.

That year was 1973, a time when I would have had no business on the Direct North West Face of Half Dome. Even so, I would gaze at pictures of the great streaked face and be drawn to what, in my mind, was the only route truly located upon Half Dome's north wall. "The Direct" peaked on the very summit, at a huge overhang called "The Visor." From The Visor it fell straight down, its course delineated by a 2,000-foot open book whose left wall was itself a library of smaller dihedrals and cracks. These cracks are the most magnificent line on one of North America's greatest walls.

Prior to 1963, when the Direct Route on the North West Face of Half Dome was first ascended, much history had already occurred on the periphery of this big wall. When the Regular North West Face Route was first climbed in 1957 by Royal Robbins, Mike Sherrick, and Gerry Gallwas, it was the longest, most difficult big wall climb in North America. When the same route was free climbed by Jim Erickson, Art Higbee, and Earl Wiggins in 1976, it held a similar position, that of the longest, most difficult big wall free climb on the continent (VI, 5.12a). These climbs opened a door of belief for climbers of each generation. The 1957 ascent proved that it was reasonable for humans to be up there at all, to thrive for days on such a forbidding and sheer face. The 1976 ascent showed that huge walls could be climbed completely free.

When viewing the great face of Half Dome, its form at first appears to be perfect, but, after a moment's viewing, its arc is unbalanced by a huge buttress hugging the left side of the mountain. This giant buttress is two-thirds as high as the great wall. While the immense face of Half Dome appears flawlessly sheer, the buttress is broken and craggy. The 1957 Regular Route meanders up sheltered cracks and corners, up narrow grooves and around the same sorts of blocky points one might find on an alpine ridge. It is this less than monolithic character and the large and numerous ledges and nooks that, to modern-day climbers, makes the Regular Route a very different physical and psychological undertaking than a climb of the sheer main wall.

While I share a mid-1990s view that the Regular Route on the North West face is, for half of its height, not on the main wall, and therefore not on "the dome," this is not intended to denigrate either the extremely significant history or the mental and physical breakthroughs of the ascents that took place on this truly great climb. For the visionary climbers who first met

The initial 400 feet of the climb follows a crack system called Crescent Arch. Paul (wearing yellow) is seen climbing into the wide crack early on in the climb.

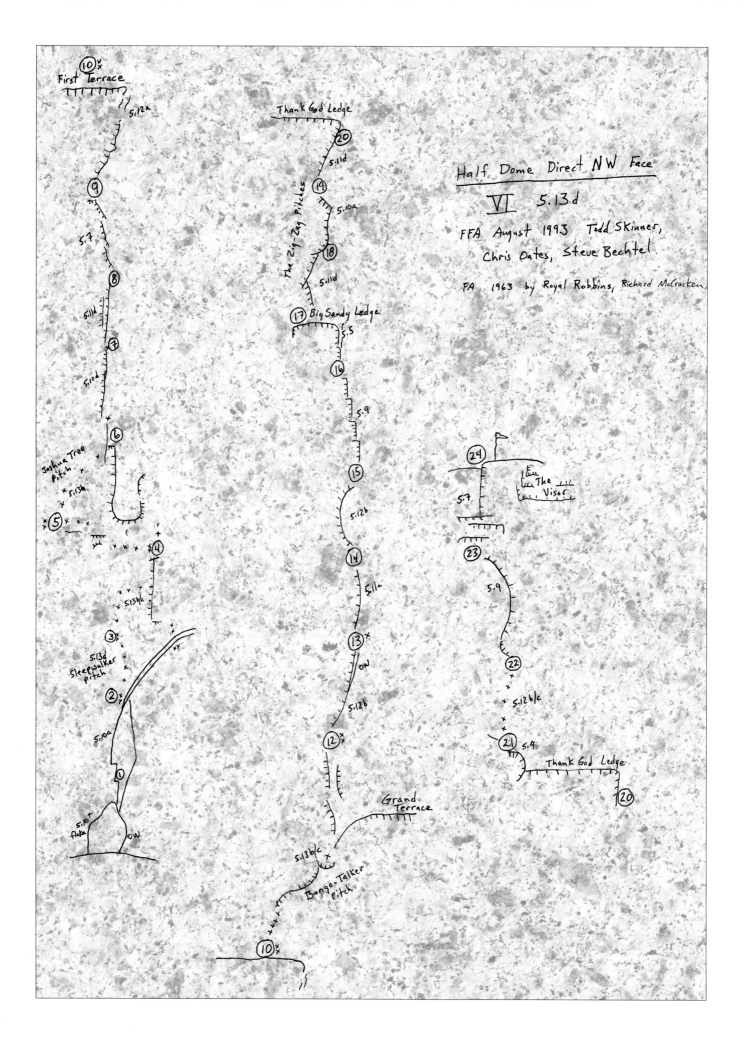

First Terrace

⑩ ✗✗

5.12a

⑨

5.7

⑧

5.11d

⑦

5.10d

⑥ ✗

Joshua Tree Pitch

✗ 5.13a

✗ ⑤ ✗✗

✗ ✗ ✗ ④ ✗

5.13b/c

③ ✗

✗✗

5.13d Sleepwalker Pitch

✗

② ✗

5.10a

①

5.10 flake ✗

OW

Thank God Ledge

⑳

5.11d

⑲

The Zig-Zag Pitches

5.10a

⑱

5.11d

⑰ Big Sandy Ledge

5.5

⑯

5.9

⑮

5.12b

⑭

5.11c

⑬ ✗

OW

5.12b

⑫ ✗✗

Grand Terrace

5.13b/c ✗

Bongo Talker Pitch

✗✗✗

⑩ ✗✗

Half Dome Direct NW Face

Ⅵ 5.13d

FFA August 1993 Todd Skinner, Chris Oates, Steve Bechtel.

FA 1963 by Royal Robbins, Richard McCracken

㉔

The Visor

5.7

㉓

5.9

㉒

✗

5.12b/c

✗

㉑ 5.4

Thank God Ledge

⑳

the challenges and for those who remained on the ground, the overall length and height were what made it noteworthy. Especially in 1957. For Gallwas, Robbins, and Sherrick, the psychological burden of climbing anywhere on this side of Half Dome was a tremendous achievement; it was easily the most spectacularly difficult climb in North America.

Sometime around 1983, I began to look into the possibility of free climbing The Direct. Clandestine queries of climbers still into direct aid climbing suggested that although extremely difficult, the route might go . . . except for two pitches. Everyone with whom I visited spoke of a section of the climb involving a bolt ladder, and a pendulum, as well as pin-scar climbing that could very well shut down a free climb. They also vaguely remembered "something weird, high up." I researched every topo and old photos of the wall and, without seeing it up close, became convinced that it would "go."

Finally, in late May 1993, twenty years after I had used the picture of Royal on my dorm room door, Todd Skinner and I were driving toward Yosemite and a long-awaited bout with the Direct North West Face of Half Dome.

W E HAD ARRANGED TO MEET Galen Rowell in a little town near the west entrance to The Valley, but after racing from Wyoming, nonstop through spring blizzards, it was 10:00 p.m. and we were two hours late. It was pouring rain in the parking lot that was our appointed meeting place, and after a headlamp-assisted search, we found tacked onto a you-are-here sign a soggy note written on stationery from a Kathmandu hotel: "Where in the hell are you? We waited from 6:00 until 8:00 p.m. and have gone back to the city. If you ever get here, meet us there."

We weren't surprised that Galen's enthusiasm had gotten the better of him. Anyone who knows Galen is aware that part of him is still ten years old and that he can't sit around waiting; he always must be going, looking, looking . . . and he was gone. It is certain that this is the very reason he has succeeded in

As this topo map indicates, The Direct is certainly well named. With the exception of the swoop of the Crescent Arch and the flourishes added by the 5.13 variations, the climbing route is no challenge to follow— but a formidable challenge to free climb.

climbing and in photography, while others have failed. Galen is a perpetual motion machine. To those who know him, this indefatigable energy combined with great talent have been the Rowell trademark.

Eventually, we arrived in Yosemite and were helping the horsepackers load our gear for the seven-mile transit to a high camp near the shoulder of Half Dome. It quickly became apparent that even though these fellas *looked like* the horse-packing wranglers back home, they were Californians, and we

Classic climbing on a classic wall. This shot shows Nancy Feagin leading the 5.10 moves at the start of the second pitch.

were at the mercy of their capitalistic whim. Had we been the 300-pounders who chug out the doors of forty-foot Winnebagos and who regularly hire these wranglers and their horses to take them as far as the start of the cables trail up Half Dome, there would have been no problem. We wanted to have the equivalent of one fat man's weight of equipment packed in, but the Californios informed us that their horses could only carry seventy-five pounds apiece. I had never before seen a horse blush, but the whole string turned pink as those boys implied that their horses were sissies.

The first night at shoulder camp was spent with a large crew who were moving up and down fixed lines on the regular route. This outfit was a group of volunteers replacing fixed gear, and were a colorful lot headed by a bushy-bearded character we immediately dubbed "the wall grizzly." His strongman was a rusty-haired dynamo from the Red River Gorge, a manimal able to hand-drill four-inch-deep, three-eighth-inch holes in less than five minutes; then, for a rest, haul 300-pound bags of water up two pitches barehanded—and then go back to drilling at his frenetic pace. His endurance wasn't perfect, though; he could sustain that rate for only twelve hours at a stretch.

The lot of us were sitting around a pleasant communal fire and enjoying the usual climbers' campfire talk. After many hours we were all lulled to drowsiness by the warmth of the fire. Someone was passing around a tub of peanut butter and some crackers when one of the crew elbowed the shadow sitting next to him. "Just a minute, dammit—I haven't even gotten any myself." At the next, more violent nudge, he turned to accost the rude scoundrel who had this time nearly knocked the tub out of his hands. He shrieked, the peanut butter and crackers caromed into the night, and barefooted, he lept into and through the fire and ran screaming into the night. For a thousandth of a second, everyone marveled at this outburst . . . but then we recognized the black bear who had hunkered down, joining our circle to share in the food. During the next split second, the formerly relaxed scene transformed into a just-kicked beehive. Everybody leapt straight up into the air

The climbers were fascinated to note that the wall at their backs mirrored in every detail the features in front of them.

and when they came down, followed the screamer into and over the fire, running in circles, hollering; "Bear! Bear! Bear!" as if they were the only ones with the ability to recognize a bruin that had been sitting next to them.

THE NEXT MORNING, Todd and I carried gear down to the base of the climb. Galen and another photographer friend carried packs filled with photographic paraphernalia. This would be the first foray to the wall for Todd and me, but Galen had bittersweet memories of the place from thirty years before . . .

In a 1993 article published in *Outdoor Photographer* and the Spanish climbing magazine *Desnivel*, Galen wrote:

> I had climbed other routes on all of Half Dome's faces, but never "The Direct" because of what happened there in 1963. Back then, a top climber and mountain photographer, Ed Cooper, invited me to join him to attempt a new direct route up Half Dome's Northwest Face. I'd just climbed the only other route on the face that began along the easier left edge and felt honored to be asked on a major new climb at the tender age of 22. Unfortunately, I had a final at U.C. Berkeley a week after Ed wanted to start. "That's okay," he told me. "We're going to spend a few days fixing ropes up blank areas on the lower face. We'll come down and go on the wall to stay when you return."

> . . . As we began climbing, the part of the lower face that most interested me defied my attempts at photography. We were the first humans to reach The Crescent Arch, a giant crack a few hundred feet above the ground that slowly widened until we could squeeze inside. Higher, it became a chimney that we could bridge with our backs and feet. Instead of disappearing into the dark depths like other chimneys, this crack ended abruptly against a smooth wall parallel with the main cliff in just eight feet. I hammered wide pitons for safety into the cracks that completely separated the back wall from the outer rock upon which we were climbing and wrote my eerie conclusion

Todd is seen climbing eight feet inside Crescent Arch, which was formed when a colossal sheet of granite detached from the main wall and slumped downward a few feet.

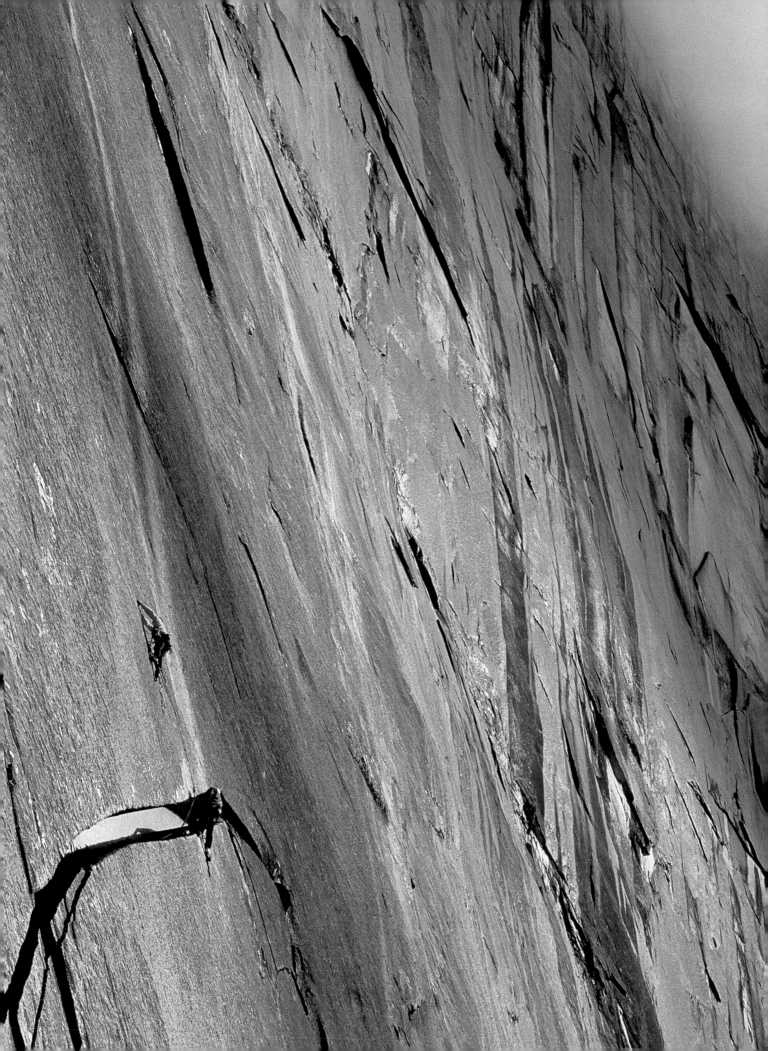

in my diary: "Here is the Half Dome face of the future, fully cleaved and waiting patiently, be it one or 100,000 years until it gleams for a geological moment in the noonday sun."

The top of the curving arch merged into blank vertical granite. We saw no natural cracks in which to place pitons, so I hand-drilled a row of quarter-inch expansion bolts spaced a few feet apart to attach ladder-like slings for direct aid. I never imagined that in 30 years climbing would advance so far that I'd be photographing people trying to free-climb this section with a safety rope clipped to my old bolts.

After my final exam, we returned to see Royal Robbins, the top rock climber of the times, climbing well above our high point with Dick McCracken. They made the first ascent in five continuous days, using the bolts I'd placed for direct aid and justifying their appropriation of our route as a single, ground-up effort in better style without the umbilical cord of the ropes we fixed on the lower face.

Ed Cooper vanished. Weeks later, he sent me a disheartened note from Manhattan, saying that he'd given up climbing for good and taken a desk job. Notably, he didn't say he was giving up outdoor photography. Although he kept his promise about hard climbing, he soon couldn't hack the city and returned west to become one of the most published large-format, color landscape photographers of the '60s and '70s. He influenced my future in 1969 by looking at some of my best Kodachromes and telling me, "You could make a living at this."

Thus, 30 years to the month after our aborted climb, I eagerly set aside all of June to join Todd Skinner and Paul Piana to attempt the first free-climb of "The Direct" using ropes for safety only. At 52, I wouldn't be free-climbing the hardest sections, but I could lead the more moderate rope lengths and take photographs of the best big-wall free climbers in the world pushing their limits to new highs.

The wall was burnished with streaks of water from the summit snows. Sorting gear near the base of the wall, Todd expressed his concern that the water streaks might hamper free climbing. Galen's photographer friend, having seen the

Todd belaying Paul on the first day of the climb. Paul is aiding toward the end of the pitch so that a top rope can be rigged from which the climbers might find a way to free climb the moves directly above the belay.

A view of Paul top-roping on what became the crux of the entire climb. Of this pitch, Paul said, "It was the most frustrating bit of climbing I had ever encountered."

to me that this key to achieving success would be a purgatory of sleepless nights and razorblade nightmares. I became increasingly dejected, as apparently I was, deep in my heart, not willing to commit to such an extended siege of this wall. I had never before encountered such an unrelentingly difficult slab, and I knew that even though The Direct was on a north-facing wall, the summer heat would be a negative factor and that even more time would be needed to succeed.

To date I had not shirked from projects requiring extended periods of time to live and to work out the solutions to free climbing on big walls. This 180-foot color change, which was always from 89 to 93 degrees in steepness, was the mind-killer. Todd was insistent that it wouldn't be as hard as I believed. He said it would be no harder than 5.13d. I bluntly replied, "You're dreamin'." From then on, Todd referred to the pitch as The Sleepwalker.

Because of the difficulties in free climbing a mere color change, we aided through and climbed to the 1,100-foot level, where there is a ledge system about fifty feet long named First Terrace. Above First Terrace was a diagonal series of hanging flakes leading up and to the right. These flakes led to a more spacious ledge called the Grand Terrace. (The hollow-sounding flakes in between the terraces were the "something weird" in discussions of years before and would eventually become known as the Bongo Talker pitch.)

At the far left side of the First Terrace, we heaved up 1,100 feet of fixed ropes and tied them together so that we could inaugurate a series of crazy pendulums. With this single strand we began scribing lines of latitude across the streaked seas of Half Dome's granite. These swinging sessions allowed us to chart several potential paths up the Half Dome wall between Arcturus and The Direct. We spent many days swinging over to

I was drowning in a vast and deep personal quandry. All sorts of real and imagined pressures had me spinning in a vortex of what normally would have been small individual concerns. And so, The Sleepwalker pitches became the blackest shadow in my nightmare.

At this point, we had been on this route for over twenty days. I kept thinking of my son, who, if I remained on this wall, would not be able to travel out west to share his school break with me. I kept thinking of the summer days swiftly passing and of all the usual haunts in which I enjoyed establishing new climbs of tremendous difficulty and great aesthetic beauty. Memories of the winds that sweep the ridges and walls of The Wild Iris played a siren song, recalling the joys of short, brutish climbs. The Black Hills Needles punctuated my dreams during the day and night—visions of thin spires bristling out of the forests and hillsides of my favorite place on earth. In the Black Hills, just five days before Todd and I drove west to Yosemite, Heidi Badaracco and I shared a remarkably perfect week of climbing new routes; and then, in the company of our closest friends, we were married among the trees and rocks.

The grass on the other side of the fence was not only greener, it was neon, screaming green. It was too much for me to bear.

In this shot of Todd working on The Sleepwalker pitch, it is possible to detect a subtle textural change that forms a vertical swath. Even poor holds would have been welcome on this section of the wall.

THE NEXT MORNING, tied into the anchors atop The Sleepwalker pitches, I sat hunched in my harness. Uncertainty and dissatisfaction seemed so heavy that I was crushing myself trying to choose between what I wanted now, and what I had wanted for years. Todd was busy below me, making even better progress top-roping, and he soon climbed up to our belay.

"Okay, now it's your turn," Todd said. "You're gonna love that step into the shallow dihedral!"

"No. I'm not climbing."

"Yeah, it's hot alright; drink some water and you'll feel better in a bit. Maybe I'll take another spin," said Todd, who misunderstood what I was saying. He began relacing his shoes.

What I said must have been a stabbing: "No, I'm not

ho
th

g

Eleven hundred feet up the wall is a 5.13a series of hollow-sounding flakes which Todd called the "Bongo Talker" pitch.

Here, the flakes suddenly ended, at which point an extremely committing, dynamic move—executed with precision, was necessary to span the gap. This sequence shows Todd winding up and throwing the dyno.

Nancy possessed all the skills necessary for a slot on the team. More important than skill, Nancy manifested a calm, fun-loving demeanor.

The only thing Nancy lacked was time. Upon agreeing to join Todd, she told him about long-standing plans that would allow her to contribute only twenty days to the effort. Elated, no doubt, by the good fortune of landing such a strong partner, as well as worrying that he would lose her, Todd probably assured Nancy that, long before her deadline, they would be

When Galen returned to photograph Todd and Nancy, they decided "against almost all hope, to begin the final push." In this wild perspective of the fourth pitch, Todd is leading while Nancy, for the moment, has put aside her crossword puzzle.

celebrating their success with dinner and wine at the Ahwanee Lodge. And so, up to Half Dome base camp they went.

I have heard little of these twenty days from either Todd or Nancy. Due to Nancy's great, good humor, there is little drama to share. Rather than be described, the story can best be seen, in several Rowell photos. When Galen (who had tired of waiting and had gone back to the city and to other photo adventures) arrived several weeks later to take some photos, Todd and Nancy decided, against almost all hope, to begin the final push. Needless to say, Todd's wildest dreams did not yet include success on The Sleepwalker pitch, and so Galen photographed them working the route. Images were captured of Nancy powering up spectacular and difficult crack-climbing pitches and enduring belaying sessions of ultra-marathon longevity. Throughout, Todd's face carries the burden of the quest, while Nancy wears her trademark smile as she climbs, or endures hours belaying by working on crossword puzzles she had taped to the wall.

During this period of the climb, Todd took a break from the first Sleepwalker pitch and solved the difficulties of The Bongo Talker pitch, which is between the First and Grand Terraces: a series of hollow, hanging flakes that culminate in a tremendous, six-foot-long, dynamic lunge. Eventually Nancy's tenure as Todd's partner was up and she left to pursue other long-anticipated climbing plans. In one of the deepest granite oceans on the planet, Todd was adrift in a sargasso sea of potential climbing partners. Yosemite Valley is a mecca for the world's climbers, and it is a simple matter to obtain a partner for short climbs or even for long aid climbs. However, a *great* partner is one of the most important and most frequently overlooked "tools" in a climber's bag of tricks. Obviously, a partner for a climb like the freeing of The Direct on Half Dome would have to possess great skill at a variety of free-climbing techniques and be willing and able to exploit these skills on many of the climb's pitches. Even more important than sharing great climbing skill, however, is being something as poetic sounding as "kindred spirits."

This hair-raising photo inadvertently creates the illusion that Todd is untied and is merely holding the rope. Never fear — his tie-in was secure; it was the hand- and footholds that were not.

Todd invited his friends, Steve Schneider and Scott Franklin, who are two of America's best free climbers. They both possess a wide variety of skills that have served them well on extremely difficult climbs. However, as each person's abilities and talents are unique, so are their personalities, and therein lay the major problem when Steve and Scott signed on. Todd and I (usually) made the ideal partnership: we share the same climbing goals, we think alike when it comes to the philosophy of climbing, and we know each other extremely well after fifteen years as climbing partners.

The desperation of climbing a color change is seen on Todd's face in this view of the 5.13d crux pitch.

Unfortunately for Todd and Steve and Scott, this Half Dome crew was not a good match. Now the necessity of leading the remaining crux pitches, combined with the even more trying problem of getting along with a poorly balanced team, was robbing Todd of sleep. While they were climbing together, Todd finally managed to red-point the crux of the route--The Sleepwalker. Scott solved another 5.13 puzzle by climbing a desperate traversing pitch. Steve had been working, the second nightmare--a 5.13 c lead into and up the foot-deep dihedral.

After gaining momentum by freeing The Sleepwalker pitch, a problem arose with scheduling. This involved waiting for Galen to complete another photo shoot, as Todd felt that photo documentation was important to his career. He suggested that either the team free the route twice--once right away and again for Galen, who had arranged for a *Life* magazine article-- or delay the final push until Galen's return, five days later. Scott assumed that since Todd would be making a lot of money, he should be compensated $750.00 per day for the extra days he would be required to spend on the climb. This led to a less than friendly argument in which tensions boiled to the point where Scott left the team and Steve decided to go as well.

tion. From hundreds of feet above, Steve watched Chris's Chicken-Little-the-Sky-Is-Falling, air-raid evasion maneuvers. Steve watched the tumbling shapes soar down the dihedrals, scraping loose large rocks which joined in the deadly plummet. He watched as the bodies *whooosshed* past and only then realized he had been narrowly missed by two haul bags, of which a Korean team on Big Sandy Ledge had traumatically and incompetently lost track. Poor Chris changed directions one too many times because, on his last reversal, he was clipped by one of the haul bags.

The great, white, brawler swung a hell of a haymaker and knocked Chris out for the count. Unconscious, Chris was still seeing stars when Steve, wanting to see just how thin a Canadian sport climber could get, completed his speed rappels to the base. This time, Todd had chosen well, and was correct in his assessment that Canadians are an unusually robust species. Todd said that he knew it was common for hundred-grain bullets to bounce, with no ill effect, off iron clad Canadians, but was a little surprised when an eighty-pound haul bag merely ricocheted off of Chris's shoulder.

From left to right, Steve Bechtel, Chris Oates, and Todd. For any difficult venture, a solid team is essential. It goes without saying that skill is a necessary ingredient, but good friends with the proper spirit are imperative.

This shot captures the essence of the crux of The Direct on Half Dome. After months of trying, and just inches from the belay and success on this 5.13d pitch, Todd slipped and took a relatively long fall.

Dejected and slumped on the rope, Todd hung in leaden silence for a long, long time. He has often said that "success has two definitions: winning, and not losing." Like the champion he is, he accepted the failure and pulled together his resolve to give his best again and again. Eventually, he did not fall.

A few minutes later, Chris was up on wobbly feet, spoiling for a fight. He had suffered only torn shoulder muscles, rasp-like abrasions, a world-class headache, and a broken finger. (Steve later would proclaim it a miracle that Chris survived, while other Canadians, who heard of the accident, seemed horribly ashamed that one of theirs could be knocked out by such a trivial missile.) In any case, Chris was slow to ascend the fixed lines the next morning.

What could Todd find so interesting about the sole of a shoe? Fingertips and tiptoes—these are the only points of contact on severe face climbs, and each must be kept in good repair.

Soon after that, haul bags and climbers ceased to fall from the sky, as Todd red-pointed the second hardest pitch of the climb. He wrote:

> On the 61st day, just short of forever, I broke through the last hard 5.13 pitch and we moved onto the wall that night. Steve and Chris did most of the 5.11's and 5.12's that remained and I stepped in only when I was tired of jumaring. Two days later, we arrived at the summit looking rough and wild-eyed, out of food and water and delighted to simply be alive. There had been five pitches of 5.13, five more of 5.12, and seven of the other fourteen had been 5.11. We were met on the top by beautiful women who gave us candy and lemonade as payment to be in our summit photo. We laughed loudly, kissed women we'd never met, lamented not having pistols to shoot in the air, and generally acted like Cowboys ought to after completing the first free ascent of the most difficult Big Wall in the world!

With the successful first free ascent of the Direct North West Face of Half Dome, Todd had completed the great goal which he and I had set for ourselves so many years ago. Much more than his vast climbing talent, it was his immense store of tenacity that brought him success. Normally, I, too, am able to reach inside myself and make the mental adjustments necessary to perform well on a project of this nature; but not this time. Maybe if we had chosen a different summer or a different season . . . maybe if Heidi and I had not been married only a few days before I left. For me, there are still too many maybes.

Heinrich Harrer once said, "It is a bad thing when the band plays before you set off for the mountain." The band seemed especially loud to me, as Galen was looking forward to a potential *Life* magazine article profiling our free-climbing successes on the four great walls, and all three of us had been affected by the loud brass. Galen was excited with the magazine contract. Todd was happy with the prospect of a *Life* cover photo. And I could not find a reason with which to be content. I am certain that, by my leaving, I prolonged the time it took to free climb The Direct. I also regret all of the turmoil that my decision had caused Todd. Galen was disappointed and angry

not to have returned to the wall in time to participate in the final push. Todd was disappointed to have been abandoned in the middle of a fight and with the thumbtack-studded game of musical chairs he was forced to play with some partners.

With Steve Bechtel belaying and Chris Oates looking on, Todd jams a little finger into a pin scar.

IT OFTEN AMAZES ME HOW strange all of the various climbing games really are. Sometimes, for a few seconds, I catch myself shaking my head at them, thinking that there is really no point. But, as we do not need to climb cliffs to *survive* on this planet, some of us desperately need these climbing games in order to *live* on this planet. We need the struggle, not so much for the obvious challenge the rock provides, but to bring forth the excellent adversary of self with which we are forced to contend. Over the years, Todd and I have battled and vanquished not mere cruxes, but fought the doubts and weaknesses within ourselves.

From scrappy little crags, to the Direct Route on the North West Face of Half Dome, we have warred against slick-sided finger jams, with doubts and with fears. Through it all, we have gained the strengths and the confidence to challenge further goals on the rocks and other areas of life. Since we choose to continually learn from all experiences, we always win. Maybe these climbing games we play have only served to train us for further adventures on the rocks. Or maybe they have trained us for the nonclimbing challenges of life. Probably, these climbs have trained us for both.

HALF DOME POSTSCRIPT

SINCE THE SUMMER OF '93, the Half Dome summer, both Todd and I have gone on to other climbs. Mostly we have concentrated on making first ascents near our homes in Lander, Wyoming. However, since then, Heidi Badaracco and I have made the first free ascent of the Pan American Wall on Mexico's El Gran Trono Blanco (V, 5.12c/d) and Todd, along with Jeff Bechtel, Bobby Model, and Mike Lilygren, has recently succeeded on the most difficult, high-

By freeing this route, Todd also succeeded in the quest we began years ago: to free climb what we consider to be the premier big walls on the continent.

Sweet success after sixty-three days of relentless effort, Todd, Galen, Chris, and Steve relax in the evening sun. The successful free ascent of The Direct North West Face of Half Dome is easily the most difficult big wall free climb in North America.

altitude, big wall free climb in the world, with the Cowboy Direct on Pakistan's Nameless Tower (VII, 5.13a).

Occasionally, our focus on what we wish to achieve within the context of free climbing switches between list to list of dream climbs and of places to visit. This not only provides a hedge against experiencing a burnout of desire, but intensifies the feeling that "there is no tomorrow." This impending deadline urges us to appreciate whatever climbing opportunity is at hand and to keep trying our hardest.

Life magazine did use Galen's photos of the first free ascents of the four big walls portrayed in this book. The coverage was a rare mainstream look at a sport most of America doesn't understand and erroneously considers a stunt. The photos *Life* selected were typical of Galen Rowell's work, beautiful, and evocative. It was nice coverage and, more than any prior media attention, the *Life* story solicited a tremendous response to us and to our sport, as well as prompting a slew of slide show bookings. I am proud of the positive and motivational message I have tried to convey about our sport and our souls.

EPILOGUE

WHERE WILL I BE IN FIVE YEARS? I do have a pretty good idea about where I'll find myself. Both Todd and I have agendas which are written down and which we deliberately pursue. My list of free-climbable big walls, shorter climbs and boulder problems, as well as foreign lands to visit is not exactly static; but I do actively strive to make my dreams come true.

In addition to climbing, I have many other interests. There are other books to write, films to make, and business opportunities to pursue. I'm committed to our home of Lander, Wyoming, and also to our home state of Wyoming. Since moving to Lander to develop and enjoy the outstanding sport climbing at local dolomite cliffs like The Wild Iris, Sinks Canyon, and Baldwin Creek, Todd and I have both entered into the business community.

With partners, Todd has opened Wild Iris Mountain Sports, Lander's full-service climbing shop. In addition, through "Extreme Connection," Todd has embarked upon a successful career as a corporate motivational speaker. Both Todd and I have further contributed to the industry by working as spokesmen and as technical consultants. My wife Heidi and I have opened "The Gravity Club," a state-of-the-art, indoor climbing gym, as well as, traveling as manufacturers representatives for "Five-Ten" climbing shoes and to present slideshows and training seminars. It seems like the more we do, the more potential we recognize.

Whether or not the sport will follow, I have very definite ideas about when, where, and what I want to be climbing. Some of the climbs that both Todd and I have done have influenced the direction that modern rock climbing is going. I can only write that my list of goals is a personal choice. I tend to listen to my own climbing muse.

Once, during a long stretch of tipi living, I was living off of enthusiasm for climbing, rather than regular meals. My mother, not understanding my motivation, asked, "What are you going to be when you grow up?" and I could only answer, "Happy!"

I believe the same is true for Todd. We are happiest when we are out on the rocks, enthusiastically striving toward the goals each of us set for ourselves so long ago. Enthusiasm is the greatest asset, and while I am very proud of all we have achieved, I'm even more excited about plans for future adventures. The only thing lacking is time and, realizing this, I've vowed to live my life like a thrown knife. So far, I have been true to myself and have always been right on target.

Anything merely dreamed and untried is wasted, while a great thing only half-tried cheats one's potential. I hope that some day, a young climber with dreams will look at these photos and read of these adventures and be inspired to make his or her dreams become reality. The stories of these big wall free climbs and the adventures that led up to them are, I hope, interesting and inspiring. However, Henry Ford once said, "History is bunk." One's own history is the most important to monitor, since today will be tomorrow's history. I hope all readers of *Big Walls*, as they blow out the candles on their hundredth birthday cake, can look back and be content that they used their time to the fullest.

Everyone else's definition of "life" must wait. There is no tomorrow!

APPENDIX: FAVORITE CLIMBS

THIS IS HARDLY A COMPLETE LIST of first ascents for either Todd or me, but it is a testimonial to our belief that an important contribution to the sport of climbing is the establishment of new routes. The criterion for climbs listed here is simply that these are our favorites.

FA = free ascent

FFA = first free ascent

FAVORITE ROUTE LIST—PAUL PIANA

BIGHORN MOUNTAINS, WYOMING

Great Spirit V, 5.12a. July 1996. Lost Twin Lakes Cirque, with Heidi Badaracco

Coup Stick IV, 5.10d. August 1996. Lost Twin Lakes Cirque, with Pete deLannoy

BLACK HILLS, SOUTH DAKOTA

RUSHMORE NEEDLES

Bugs Tomorrow 5.10d. 1989, with Heidi Badaracco

The Gossamer 5.7. 1989, with Heidi Badaracco, Jacob Valdez, Amy Whisler

Critical Crewcut 5.12c. 1989, with Heidi Badaracco

Yuppie Warfare 5.12b. 1989, with Heidi Badaracco

The Dykes Next Door 5.10d. 1989, with Heidi Badaracco

Girlie Man 5.12c. 1989, with Heidi Badaracco

Beetlejuice 5.12b. 1990, with Mike Johnston

Blue Mascara 5.10c. 1989, with Heidi Badaracco

Jacknife Matinée 5.13a. 1989, with Todd Skinner. We scoped, drilled, and we both led it in one afternoon.

Tomcat Tracer 5.13a. 1989, followed by Todd Skinner

12 White Sticks 5.12a. 1989, followed by Gary Geraths

Forbidden Colors 5.13b. 1989, with Heidi Badaracco
Madam Mohawk 5.11a. 1989, with Heidi Badaracco
Bulldyke 5.10a. 1989, with Heidi Badaracco
Punky's Dilemma 5.11. 1989, with Gary Geraths
The Real Roxanne 5.13a. 1989, followed by Todd Skinner with
    Jacob Valdez
Slang 5.12a. 1989
Boylesque 5.11c. 1990, with Heidi Badaracco
Storybook Kisser, 5.12a. 1990, with Heidi Badaracco
Snakebite Evangelist 5.13a. November 1990, with
    Heidi Badaracco
Black Elk Speaks 5.12a. 1991, with Heidi Badaracco
Remnants of a Fine Woman 5.12c. 1993, Heidi Badaracco led first

SYLVAN LAKE NEEDLES
Wildman Traverse 5.7. 1971, with Ken Jones and Chris Field
Sandberg Peak 5.8 November 1972
Spiro Staircase, 5.9+. August 1974, Bob Kamps led
Woman of 1000 Years 5.5. 1974
Indian Giver 5.8. Late 1970s, with Paul Muehl
Sex Never Did This to My Hands 5.9. 1978, with Paul Muehl,
    Bob Archbold
Every Whichway But Loose 5.11a. 1979, led by Pete deLannoy,
    with Paul Muehl
Call Girl 5.6. Spring 1980, with Todd Skinner, Gregg Waterman,
    and others
Right Wing of Smaug 5.11b. Early 1980s, with Paul Muehl
Worm Tongue 5.8. Early 1980s
Of Quartz It Goes 5.7. Early 1980s, with Paul Muehl
Goldline 5.9. July 1980
Julius Seizure 5.10d. July 1980, with Kevin Bein, Barb Devine
Rough and Crumble 5.10a. July 1980, with Kevin Bein,
    Barb Devine
Paul's Bunyon 5.10. August 1980, with Paul Muehl
A Farce To Be Reckoned With 5.11. August 1980, Kevin Bein led
A Cold Girl Will Kill You 5.12aR+. Mid 1980s, Todd Skinner led
Strawberry Waterfall 5.11c. 1985
The Terminator 5.12a. 1985, led by Eric Doub, with Paul Muehl
Finger Peak, Knock, Knock 5.10bX. 1985, with Eric Doub,
    Pete deLannoy

Buckshot Eyes and a Purple Heart 5.11a. Autumn 1990, with
    Paul Muehl
Lean and Mean 5.9+. Early 1990s, with Herb and Jan Conn,
    Paul Muehl
Rat Race 5.6. Early 1990s, with Herb and Jan Conn,
    Paul Muehl
Fearless Bleeder, 5.11aR. May 1992, with Heidi Badaracco,
    Cindy Tolle, Pete deLannoy
Every Whichway But Kamps 5.12bR. May 1993, with
    Heidi Badaracco

BOULDER, COLORADO
Hey Slick 5.7. 1986
The East Ironingboard Crack 5.7. 1986
Hot Spit 5.11b. 1987
The Big Picture 5.12b. 1987, with Dan Michael
Camouflage 5.12c. 1987, with Dan Michael
Wasabi 5.12c. 1987, with Dan Michael, Mark Sonnenfeld
Raptor in Cellophane 5.10+. 1987
P.S. I'm Blonde 5.12a. 1987, with Brett Ruckman
Velvet Elvis 5.11a. 1987, with Brett Ruckman
Hunka Hunka Burnin' Love 5.10b. June 1989, with
    Heidi Badaracco
Stars at Noon 5.12d. May 1988, with Pete deLannoy
Sinatra's World 5.13a. June 1989

BUTTON ROCK AREA, NEAR LYONS, COLORADO
Big-Big Monkey Man 5.12b. 1985, with "Nitro" Petro
Introducing Meteor Dad 5.10d. 1985, with Catherine Freer
Finger Tattoo 5.12a. August 1985
Pretty Blue Gun 5.12a. August 1985
Spy Dust 5.10d. 1985
Tigers in Lipstick 5.10. 1985, with Suzanne Jackson
Hitler's Sex Life 5.11c. 1985, with Matt Lavender
Gestapo Mega 5.11dX. 1985
Fat Girls on Mopeds 5.11d. 1985, with Jeff Achey
Green Slab 5.9X. 1985
Infamous Pink Thunderbird 5.11c. 1986, with
    George Bracksieck

CANADA

The Great Canadian Knife VI, 5.13a. August 1992, with Todd
    Skinner, Galen Rowell. Cirque of the Unclimbables, Logan
    Mountains, Northwest Territories, Canada. Mount Proboscis.

CODY, WYOMING

She's So Teenage 5.10a. March 1984, with Kirt Cozzens
Thunderbirds Are Go 5.9+. March 1984, with Todd Cozzens

DEVILS TOWER, WYOMING

Pigeon English 5.9. April 1984, with Bill Hatcher
The Best Crack in Minnesota 5.9. 1984, with Bob Cowan,
    Beth Wald, Todd Skinner
Approaching Lavender 5.11c. July 1984, with Bob Cowan,
    Todd Skinner, Beth Wald
English Beat 5.12b. July 1984, led by Todd Skinner, with
    Bob Cowan
Bloodguard 5.12a. July 1984, led by Todd Skinner, with
    Beth Wald, Bob Cowan
Nitro Express 5.12a. 1985, led by Steve "Nitro" Petro. FFA of first
    and third pitches
Daredevil Index 5.12a. June 1985, with Steve Petro

FAIRFIELD HILL, WYOMING

Doll Parts 5.11d. December 1995, with Heidi Badaracco
Our Barbies, Our Selves 5.12a. December 1995, with Heidi
    Badaracco
My Dying Bride 5.12c. March 1996, with Heidi Badaracco

HUECO TANKS, TEXAS

Save the Cows 5.10+. 1982, Todd Skinner led
Walkin' Spanish Down the Hall 5.13a. February 1991
Peewee Schwarzenegger 5.12aR. December 1991, with
    Heidi Badaracco

JOSHUA TREE, CALIFORNIA

Legolas 5.10c. February 1976
Tom Bombadil 5.7. 1976

Are You Experienced 5.11aR. 1981. First free lead with
Todd Skinner and Lisa Schassberger
Hot Knife 5.10d. Spring 1981, with Todd Skinner
Joshua Tree Verse 5.9+. Spring 1981, with Todd Skinner
On Beyond Zebra 5.8. Spring 1981

MEXICO

CABO SAN LUCAS

Gringolandia 5.11a. February 1993, with Heidi Badaracco,
Bill Hatcher, John Bernhart

CAÑON TAJO

Pan American Route V+, 5.12c/d. November 1993, with
Heidi Badaracco
White Lightning 5.10a. February 1976, led by Paul Kortopates,
with Gary Geraths
Diamonds and Rust 5.10b. February 1976, with Gary Geraths
Soft Parade 5.7. February 1976, with Gary Geraths

RUIDOSO, NEW MEXICO

Damn Perignon 5.11d. August 1982

RUMBLING BALD, NORTH CAROLINA

Blonde Svengali 5.12a. 1989

SHELF ROAD, THE BANK, COLORADO

Ice Cream Hangover 5.11b. 1987, with Colin Lantz and
Greg Robinson

SINKS CANYON, WYOMING

Blushing Crow 5.12c. March 1992
Mano a Mano 5.13a. May 1992
Confession of a Mask 5.13a. May 1994
Software 5.12c. March 1996
Mergatroid 5.12a. March 1996, with Heidi Badaracco
Happy Wheel 5.10a. April 1996, with Heidi Badaracco
Mezzmeree 5.12 b/c. April 1996, with Heidi Badaracco
Purple Galaxy 5.12a. May 1996, with Heidi Badaracco

SUCK CREEK, TENNESSEE

Jerry's Kids 5.10d. Mid 1980s, with Arno and Mark Ilgner

MOUNT LEMMON, TUCSON, ARIZONA

Swordfishtrombone 5.11c. Spring 1990, with Heidi Badaracco
Barracuda Green Point 5.11a. Spring 1990, with Heidi Badaracco

VEDAUWOO, WYOMING

Tuesday Afternoon (a.k.a. *Persistence*) 5.9+, FFA,. 1973, with
    Steve Matous
SpiderGod 5.11a. April 1979, with Kelly Thorpe
Orange Christmas 5.11a. September 1979, with Todd Skinner
    (our first new route together)
Neon Cowboy 5.10b/c. October 1979
Jimi Handtrix 5.11. Spring 1980, put up with Todd Skinner
Mick Jagged 5.11. Spring 1980, put up with Todd Skinner
Friday 13th 5.11d. September 1980, with Todd Skinner
    (FA of upper roof and FFA of entire route)
Popcorn Farce 5.10a. October 1980
Strong Love 5.11. November 1980
Silver Surfer 5.10a. 1980
Pring Fever 5.11. February 1981
Pod Awful 5.10a. April 1981
4th of July Crack 5.12a. Fall 1980, with Todd Skinner
Eleven-Cent Moon 5.11d. August 1981, with Todd Skinner
Mr. Chimp 5.11/5.12. October 1981, Todd Skinner led first
Change of Hard 5.9R. April 1982, with Suzanne Jackson
Arch Stanton 5.11dR. May 1982, Todd got the first lead. Ended at
    a hanging belay near the end of the arch.
Reading Raymond Chandler 5.12a. July 1982
Five Sleazy Creases 5.9+. July 1982
Blade Runner 5.11. July 1982, with Kevin Bein, Barb Devine
Flare Thee Well 5.11b. February 1982, with Todd Skinner
Crankenstein 5.12a. March 1982, with Todd Skinner,
    Lisa Schassberger
Brave Shadow 5.9X. 1982
Cool Jet 5.11c. June 1983, with Bill Hatcher
Cut Off My Legs and Call Me Shorty 5.10. June 1983, with
    Bill Hatcher

Japan Club 5.10. Summer 1983

Who the Heck's Charlie Creese 5.10. Summer 1983

Harder Than Your Husband 5.12c. July 1983

Cool Hand Luke 5.10d. September 1983

I'm Spartacus 5.11b. October 1983, with Todd Skinner, Beth Wald

Hello Stupid 5.10b. October 1983, with John Mattson

London Calling 5.11d. October 1983, I followed Skinner.

Flaming Blue Jesus 5.10c. 1983

Torn Curtain 5.9+. February 1984, with Bill Hatcher

Master of Sport 5.12b. June 1984

Pretty Girls with Long Knives 5.12b. I led FFA of first pitch in July 1984. In August 1984 with Hidetaka Suzuki, I followed second ascent of first pitch and first ascent of 5.10c exit crack.

What the French Girl Said 5.11a. August 1984, with Bob Cowan

Calling on You Moscow 5.11a. August 1984, with Bob Cowan

Last of the Elfin Boltmen 5.11X. 1984, with John Mattson

New Mutant 5.12d. August 1985

Light from Blue Horses 5.11c. October 1987

Whistling Jupiter 12c. 1988, with Todd Skinner, Dan Michael

Terminator Blueprint 5.12a. 1990, with Heidi Badaracco. This is Arch Stanton after I added bolts and climbed it all the way to the top of the formation.

VedauVoodoo 12c. August 1990, with Heidi Badaracco

VENEZUELA

Aratitiyope VI, 5.11 A3+. 1991. A huge granite shark fin forty miles from the equator. With Todd Skinner and a film crew.

WILD IRIS, WYOMING

God Bless John Wayne 5.12a. August 1990

Cowboy Poetry 5.12b. September 1990

Phony Express 5.12b. June 1991

Riata Man 5.13a. June 1991

Adi-Goddang-Yos 5.13a. August 1991

Mexican Rodeo 5.12c. October 1991

Atomic Stetson 5.13b. September 1992

Sleeping Thunder 5.12a. August 1993

Rattlesnake Tambourine 5.12a. 1994

Yowzah! 5.12a. 1994

Atomic Cow 5.13d. August 1995
Arapaho 5.11d. Summer 1995
Boy 5.13a. Summer 1996, with Heidi Badaracco
Burnt Beans and Coffee 5.12c. July 1996, with Heidi Badaracco
Silverbelly 5.13a. July 1996

COUNTRIES CLIMBED IN:

Canada, England, France, Germany, Mexico, Spain, Texas, Venezuela, Vietnam.

FAVORITE ROUTE LIST—TODD SKINNER

AMERICAN FORK

Burning 5.13b. 1989

BALDWIN CREEK, WYOMING

Daybreaker 5.13b. Summer 1994
Skyliner 5.13a. Summer 1994
Troubleshooter 5.13a. Summer 1994

BLACK HILLS, SOUTH DAKOTA

RUSHMORE NEEDLES
Goin' Up to Harlem with a Pistol in My Jeans 5.13b-5.14a.
    Fall 1990, with Amy Whisler
Lizzy Beams Desire 5.13d-5.14a. Fall 1990, with Amy Whisler
Jacknife Matinée 5.13a. Summer 1990, with Paul Piana
The Real Roxanne 5.13a. Summer 1990, with Jacob Valdez and
    Paul Piana
A Sioux Named Boy 5.13c. Summer 1991, with Amy Whisler

SYLVAN LAKE NEEDLES
Call Girl 5.6. 1980, with Paul Piana
A Cold Girl Will Kill You 5.12aR+. Mid 1980s. A bold lead, with
    Paul Piana.

CANYON DE CHELLEY
Spider Rock V, 5.10+. 1984, FFA with Tom Cosgriff

MOON HILL, CHINA

Black Lantern 5.13b. 1993, with Mike Tupper

Proud Sky 5.12d. 1993, with Jacob Valdez, Sam Lightner
Mickey Mao's 5.12b. 1993, with Jacob Valdez, Sam Lightner

CITY OF ROCK, IDAHO

Dolphin Dihedral 5.11. 1983, with "Royal" Robin Jones
Skinner's Roof 5.12a. 1983, with "Royal" Robin Jones
Electric Avenue 5.12a. 1983, with "Royal" Robin Jones

COCHITI, NEW MEXICO, WELDED TUFF

Fainting Imam 5.12c. Mid 1980s

COCHISE STRONGHOLD, ARIZONA

Dominatrix Without Mercy 5.12b. First Free Lead. Mid 1980s.

CODY, WYOMING

Sound as a Trout 5.11. Mid 1980s, with Cozzens brothers,
    Beth Wald

DEVILS TOWER, WYOMING

The Power That Preserves 5.12a. 1983, with Moana Roberts
Synchronicity 5.11d. 1983, with John Roshold
A Bridge Too Far 5.11d, FA. 1983, with Steve Hong,
    Mark Sonnenfeld
Surfer Girl 5.12b. 1984, with Beth Wald
Graeme's Line 5.12c. 1984, with Beth Wald, Bill Hatcher
Bloodguard 5.12d. 1984, with Paul Piana, Bob Cowan, Beth Wald
Approaching Lavender 5.11c. July 1984, led by Paul Piana and Bob
    Cowan, with Beth Wald
Let Me Go Wild 5.12b. Fall 1984, with Beth Wald
Avalon 5.12a. Fall 1984, with Beth Wald
Animal Cracker Land 5.12b. Fall 1984, with Beth Wald
English Beat 5.12b FA. July 1984, with Paul Piana, Bob Cowan
The Best Crack in Minnesota 5.9. 1984, led by Paul Piana, with
    Beth Wald and Bob Cowan
Risqué 5.12a. 1985, with Bill Hatcher, Beth Wald
Romeo Is Restless 5.10d. 1985, with Beth Wald, Bill Hatcher
Hollow Men 5.12cR/X. 1985, with Beth Wald, Bill Hatcher
See You in Soho 5.12b. 1985, with Beth Wald
Billy Bear Cranks the Rad 5.12c. 1985, led by Wild Bill Hatcher
Psychic Turbulence 5.11a. 1985, with Beth Wald, Danny Rosen

EGYPT

The Glorious Koran 5.11. 1983, with Kevin Blades, James Grey
Jeziel 5.11. 1983, with Julie
Mecca 5.11. 1983, with Julie
Wind and Sun and Sword 5.10. 1983, with Kevin Blades, James Grey
Infidel 5.10. 1983

FREMONT CANYON, WYOMING

Flared to Middlin' 5.11. 1985, with Steve Petro

GREECE

5.12 route on sea cliff with Christmas Eve bivvy on summit with Danny Rosen, 1983
Cool mile-long sea level traverse near Sparta, 1983

FIRST ASCENTS OF VARIOUS SUMMITS

GREEN RIVER MUD SPIRES, WYOMING

1960s with Bob, Courtney Skinner, through early 1980s

HUECO TANKS, TEXAS

Calling All Cows 5.10d. 1982, first lead with Paul Piana
The Gunfighter 5.13b. May 1984, with Theresa Würm
Dark Horse 5.11X. 1984
Darkness at the Edge of Town 5.11. 1983, with Beth Wald
True Sailing Is Dead 5.11. 1983, with Beth Wald
Gunfighter Direct Finish 5.11. 1985, with Beth Wald
Dos XX 5.11dR. 1980s
Secret Sharer 5.11d. 1980s, put up with Mike Head
Tarts of Horsham 5.12d. 1986
Lunar Abstract 5.12a. 1986
Big Brother Bans Bolting 5.11. Late 1980s
Shadows in the Rain 5.11. Mid 1980s
Tanks for the Mammaries 5.13a. Mid 1980s
When Legends Die 5.13a. 1987
Calling All Heroes 5.13c/d. 1988, with Mike
Cowboyography 5.13c/d. 1990, with Amy Whisler
Boy's Town 5.14a. 1991, with Sam Lightner, Jacob Valdez

JOSHUA TREE, CALIFORNIA

Are You Experienced 5.11aR. Spring 1981, led by Paul Piana, with
Lisa Schassberger
Hot Knife 5.10d. Spring 1981
Top Flight 5.10. 1983, with John Sherman
Rainy Day Dream Away 5.11+R. 1983, with Russ Raffa
Joshua Tree Verse 5.9+. Spring 1981, Paul Piana led

MEXICO

Routes climbed December 1986, with Bill Hatcher and
Les Harmon
Bo da thon 5.13b.
Toro Toro Taxi 5.12d.
Pocket Full of Pesos 5.12c.
Baquero 5.12c.

MOORE'S WALL, NORTH CAROLINA

First in Flight 5.12a. 1986, with Russel Erickson, Bill Hatcher,
Beth Wald
Stars and Bars 5.12c. 1986, with Russel Erickson, Bill Hatcher,
Beth Wald

PAKISTAN

Cowboy Direct Grade VII, 5.13a. Summer 1995, Nameless Tower,
Trango Tower Area, with Jeff Bechtel, Mike Lilygren,
Bobby Model. World's first grade VII free climb.

NEAR RUIDOSO, NEW MEXICO

Across the Bloomin' Heather 5.12a. 1983
Damn Perignon 5.11d. 1983

THAILAND

All routes climbed over two trips in 1992 and 1993 with
Mike Tupper, Sam Lightner, Jacob Valdez
Mekong Haze 5.13.
Hot Dragon 5.13d.
Sea Gypsy 5.13b.
Violence Is Golden 5.13c.
Smart with the Machete 5.9/12b.

Danger of Beauty 5.13c.
Beauty of Danger 5.13a.
Dry Ice 5.9.
Siamese Twins 5.7.

MOUNT LEMMON, TUCSON, ARIZONA

Liverpool Kiss 5.12d. Mid 1980s

VEDAUWOO, WYOMING

Orange Christmas 5.11a. September 1979, Paul Piana led
Friday 13th 5.11d. September 1980, FFA upper roof and FFA
    complete route with Paul Piana
Jimi Handtrix 5.11. Spring 1980, with Paul Piana
Mick Jagged 5.11. Spring 1980, with Paul Piana
Mr. Chimp 5.11/5.12. October 1981, with Paul Piana
4th of July Crack 5.12a. June 1981, with Paul Piana
Static Cling 5.11c. 1981, with Lisa Schassberger
Eleven-Cent Moon 5.11d. 1982, Paul Piana led. Sticky Rubber
    downrated this one.
Crankenstein 5.11d. March 1982, led by Paul Piana, with
    Lisa Schassberger.
London Calling 5.11d. October 1983, with Paul Piana
Whistling Jupiter 5.12c. Fall 1988, with Paul Piana, Dan Michael
Silver Salute 5.13a. Fall 1991, with Amy Whisler
Panther of the Weak 5.13a. 1992, with Amy Whisler

VENEZUELA

Aratitiyope VI 5.11, A3+. 1992. A huge granite shark fin forty miles
    from the equator. With Paul Piana, Monique Dalmasso,
    Kiké Arnal, Rick Ridgeway, Mike Graber, Paul Sharpe, and
    Marie Hiroz.

VIETNAM

All routes drilled with Hanoi Hilti during 1993.
Tupelov Monsoon 5.13a. With Sam Lightner and Jacob Valdez,
    plus two other routes

VIRGINIA DALE, COLORADO

Circus Circus 5.12c. Summer 1985, with Steve Petro

WASHINGTON STATE

Never-Never Crack 5.12d. 1985
City Park 5.13c. 1986

WILD IRIS, WYOMING

Rode Hard and Put Up Wet 5.12c. July 1990, with Amy Whisler
Copenhagen Angel 5.13b. August 1990, with Paul Piana
Throwin' the Houlihan 5.14a. July 1991, with Amy Whisler
Hey, Mr. Vaquero 5.12b. Summer 1992
Bronc Twister 5.13a. Autumn 1992
Gored by Inosine 5.12c. Summer 1994

WIND RIVER MOUNTAINS, WYOMING

Gannett Peak. 1979. First Winter Ascent of Wyoming's highest
    peak, with Courtney Skinner
Mount Hooker VI, 5.12a. August 1991, with Tim Toula,
    Galen Rowell, Paul Piana

YOSEMITE, CALIFORNIA

The Renegade/Stigma 5.13c. 1985
The Salathé Wall VI, 5.13b. 1988, with Paul Piana
The Direct North West Face of Half Dome VI, 5.13d. 1993,
    completed with Steve Bechtel, Chris Oates

COUNTRIES CLIMBED IN

Canada, China, Czechoslovakia, Egypt, England, France,
    Germany, Greece, Hong Kong, Ireland, Israel, Italy, Lesotho,
    Mexico, Pakistan, Poland, South Africa, Spain, Switzerland,
    Texas, Thailand, USSR, Venezuela, Vietnam.

PHOTO CREDITS